Texas Gardening

TEXAS GARDENING
Answers from the Experts

Laura C. Martin

with illustrations by the author

TAYLOR PUBLISHING COMPANY
Dallas, Texas

To my favorite Texan,
my husband, Bill Brenner

Published by Taylor Publishing Company
1550 West Mockingbird Lane
Dallas, Texas 75235
www.taylorpub.com

Library of Congress Cataloging-in-Publication Data

Martin, Laura C.
    Texas gardening : answers from the experts / Laura C. Martin.
      p.   cm.
    Includes bibliographical references.
    ISBN 0-87833-201-4
    1. Gardening—Texas. 2. Gardeners—Texas—Interviews. I. Title.
SB453.2.T4M27   1998
635'.092'2764—dc21   98-38039
                                         CIP

Printed in the United States of America
10 9 8 7 6 5 4 3 2 1

TABLE OF CONTENTS

INTRODUCTION

Ask anyone, anywhere and they will tell you: Texas is big. Everything about Texas is big. It covers an enormous physical area and includes growing regions that stretch from tropical to cold (really cold!), supporting plants as diverse as banana trees and blue spruce. The growing regions of the state are not clearly defined, for there is much overlap from one area to the next, and plants—like people—are not easily pigeonholed. Based on USDA horticultural information, though, growing zones in the state of Texas range from Zone 9 in the southern tip of the state to Zone 5 in the Panhandle.

But Texans seem to like extremes and take great pleasure in boasting of living in the coldest, or hottest, or most humid, or driest climate in the United States, and usually their boasts are well founded. These same folks also take great pleasure in showing off their magnificent gardens and the biggest, most colorful plants that they can grow in spite of the challenges of climate, soil, and general weather conditions.

The diversity of gardening challenges makes it difficult for a gardener to know just how to garden well in their particular part of Texas. Thus, the advice of regional experts becomes invaluable. As soils and climate vary, so does gardening information, and answers to questions such as when to plant and harvest, which plants to use, and how to water and mulch in any particular locale are essential to gardening successfully throughout the state.

As I traveled throughout Texas, driving (and driving and driving) from one spot to the next, I saw scenes beautiful enough to stir the soul: sweeping vistas of bluebonnets in the Hill Country; the Piney Woods of East Texas; the cacti and yucca of the high plains of the west. It was clear that the natural landscape served as inspiration for many of the gardens and manmade landscapes found throughout the state.

And what gardens are found here! From the tropical paradise at Moody Gardens in Galveston to the organic herb beds at the Festival Institute near Round Top, Texas gardens are unique and exciting, providing both education and inspiration for visitors from around the world.

The folks who make this possible, the Texas gardeners, are a diverse, dedicated, and highly talented group of people. They not only enhance the beauty of the state, they also add to the general health and welfare of the citizens of Texas. Contributions have come from people such as Bob Randall, director of Urban Harvest, dedicated to feeding the hungry and educating people about wise land use; Libbie Winston, who for many years taught folks about organic gardening and herbal crafts; Rosa Finsley, who strives to develop landscapes that make people feel grounded and connected to their roots; Michael Shoup, who has earned an international reputa-

tion for his work with antique roses; and William C. Welch; and Howard Garrett and—well, the list is long and impressive.

In *Texas Gardening* I present interviews with twenty-nine of the most dedicated, horticulturally knowledgeable individuals in Texas, although they represent only a small portion of the hundreds of outstanding gardeners in the state. Their wisdom is impressive, their accomplishments inspiring. In sharing their knowledge and answering questions that range from basic to philosophical, they have dedicated themselves to helping gardeners throughout the state create places of bounteous beauty.

In meeting these people and seeing their gardens, I met not only gardeners, but friends. There is an instant bond among people who share a love of the earth and a passion for digging in the soil, no matter where they're from or where they garden. An aphid in Atlanta is just as irritating as an aphid in Dallas, and the sweet fragrance of a newly opened rose in Georgia will warm the heart as surely as the unfolding petals of the yellow rose of Texas.

Texas Gardening

GETTING STARTED

Knowing your particular region and the growing conditions it presents is a major key to gardening successfully within the state of Texas. Finding microclimates and niches in your own particular yard or garden is also an important step in making things grow, for if you can find a spot that is protected from cold or wind or the heat of the afternoon sun, you may be able to grow things that your neighbors cannot.

Drastic changes in the weather affect gardeners in all parts of the state, and many experts admit that temperatures dropping from the seventies to the teens within a twenty-four-hour period is enough to frustrate even the most experienced gardener. Summer monsoons, extended droughts, and the sudden appearance of a "blue norther" add to the challenges of gardening in Texas. There's really no such thing as "average" in Texas. As county extension horticultur-

ist Jerry Parsons says, "If you have one foot in boiling water and one foot in ice water, on the average, you're comfortable!"

In spite of these difficulties, Texans have learned to make the most of these conditions and have established gardens of enviable productivity and breathtaking beauty. From a bountiful vegetable garden in Amarillo to the splendor of the Tyler Rose Festival, Texas gardens are among the best in the country.

The general consensus of all the experts was this: If we can do it, you can do it. They offered the following "Golden Rules of Texas Gardening":

Remember that the primary rule about gardening is to enjoy it. If you're not having fun in your garden, then why do it?

Choose plants that are naturalized or adapted to the growing region in which you live. How do you know what to plant? As Rosa Finsley suggests, "steal with your eyes." Look around you both at naturalized areas that you find beautiful and at gardens that are close to your house, whether they are public gardens or a backyard neighborhood garden.

Garden organically whenever possible. When you feel that it is necessary to use chemicals for pest control or to add fertilizers to the soil, use the least invasive and least toxic materials possible.

Be realistic about the resources—time, money, and space—you have available for your garden. Plant only what you can comfortably take care of. Most experts suggest that you start small and see how you like the world of gardening before you commit yourself to a large landscaped space.

Be a patient gardener. It takes time for plants to grow, so leave enough room for them to grow into their natural, mature state. Even though your landscape might look a little sparse at first, don't crowd your plants. If necessary, fill in with annuals or short-lived plants, and remove these as your larger plants mature.

Learn to feed the soil rather than feed the plants for a long-term healthy garden. Use the organic materials that are easily accessible to you (compost, shredded bark, etc.) and work them into the soil at least to the root level. Composting is always a good idea, though in some regions of the state it is so dry that it takes a long time for the materials to decompose.

Choose your planting site carefully and include plants that will grow well there. If a plant needs full sun, don't plant it in a shady spot. If it needs constant moisture, don't plant it where high, drying winds are a problem.

Expect to give special attention to plants that you grow in areas to which they are not native. For example, if you grow tropical plants in Houston, extra time and energy will be needed to protect them against occasional inclement weather.

Be prepared. Have a plan in mind before you start digging, and prepare the soil before you start buying. Although all gardeners are subject to impulse buying (who can resist those gorgeous flowers!), make sure that you have an appropriate site ready for them before you bring them home. Remember the old "kittens grow up to be cats" rule. Tiny little seedlings may grow up to be oak trees.

Share what you know, what you love, and what you have. If you have an abundance of fruits and vegetables, contact a nearby community garden about donating your surplus. If you know how to grow bearded iris in Amarillo, share your experiences and tricks with a local gardening group. Sharing your garden, your knowledge, and your experiences is a wonderful way to develop lifelong friendships.

PLANT NAMES

Plant nomenclature is sometimes confusing to a new gardener. These definitions should help ease the confusion:

Annuals are plants that complete a life cycle within one year. Sometimes a plant tag reads "treat as an annual." This generally applies to plants that have a longer natural life cycle, but because of climatic limitations will last only a single growing season in a particular area.

Biennials are plants that complete their growing cycle within two years. Generally, these plants, such as Sweet William, spend the first year putting down

roots. They bloom the second year and die after blooming. Sometimes, in warm regions, biennials planted from seed in early spring will produce blossoms by late summer.

Perennials are plants that live more than two years. Some perennials, such as Black-eyed Susan (*Rudbeckia hirta*), are considered "short-lived" and usually last no more than two years, but most perennials live much longer.

Herbaceous plants have soft, fleshy stems and foliage. Most annuals, biennials, and perennials are considered herbaceous plants.

Herbs are a wide variety of plants usually designated by their usefulness in cooking, crafts, or medicines.

Most, but not all, garden plants have a *common name* by which they are known. A plant may have several common names. Pansies, for example, have collected dozens of common names through the centuries, including "Kiss Me in the Pantry" and "Hearts-ease." Although sometimes confusing, these are familiar, fun names, descriptive and easy to pronounce.

To eliminate confusion, all plants have a Latin *botanical name*, composed of a genus and a species. These are written in italics, with the genus capitalized and the species in lowercase letters. (Often the genus name and the common name will be the same. For example, *Coreopsis verticillata* is commonly known as coreopsis.) Although the botanical names of plants are sometimes changed, these names are recognized throughout the world. No two different kinds of plants can have exactly the same botanical name.

Varieties describe plants within the same species that show dependable variation generation after generation. Plant varieties often occur within specific geographic ranges. Variety names are preceded by the designation "Var." and are italicized. A specific kind of mountain bluestar, for example, is identified as *Amsonia tabernaemontana* var. *montana*.

Cultivars are plants that have been hybridized or selected for certain characteristics. Cultivars, when planted from seed, may or may not stay true to the characteristics of their parents, and are thus propagated by division, stem or root cuttings, or tissue culture. Many garden plants are cultivars. The cultivar name is listed in single quotes (often preceded by the abbreviation "cvs.") and not italicized, as in *Zinnia angustifolia* 'Crystal White'. The terms "variety" and "cultivar" are often used interchangeably by gardeners.

Hybrids are plants that occur when two species or genera of plants cross-pollinate, either naturally or as a result of the work of a plant breeder. Hybrid names are designated with an "X". For example, *Anemone* X *hybrida* is a cross between two species of *Anemone*.

REGIONS OF TEXAS

The Texas Agricultural Extension Service divides the state into twelve districts. Average growing conditions are given for a town or city within each district, and quotes, tips, and advice are included for each region.

Panhandle

Texas Agricultural Extension
　Service
District 1
6500 Amarillo Boulevard, West
Amarillo, TX 79106
806-359-5401

Amarillo
Average annual precipitation:
　19 inches
Average last spring frost:
　April 17
Average first fall frost:
　October 24
Average growing season:
　190 days
Horticulture Zone: 6

Eddie Henderson, Amarillo:
Amarillo Botanical Gardens
We have a unique climate in that it is extreme. We have cold, wet winters and hot, dry summers. Gardening is a challenge for both plants and people. We can't rely on horticultural zones as indicators for selecting plant material, because the zone maps are based on averages. On the average, our weather is not so bad, but the extremes kill the plants. Cold weather here comes on quickly.
　Tips and advice: Choose plant material carefully. Amend the soil. Look for microclimates or niches in your own yard.

South Plains

Texas Agricultural Extension
　Service
District 2
Route 3
Box 213 AA
Lubbock, TX 79401-9746
806-746-6101

Lubbock

Average annual precipitation: less
than 19 inches
Average last spring frost: April 9
Average first fall frost:
November 3
Average growing season:
208 days
Horticulture Zone: 7a

James Harris, Lubbock:
Landscape Architect
In planning a garden in Lubbock,
you need to consider not only
temperature extremes (we've
gone from 70° to 7° in a single
day), but also elements such as
prevailing winds, light intensity,
light reflection, heat retention
in hard surfaces close to garden
beds, low humidity, high soil pH,
soil texture, high mineral content
of the domestic water supply, and
limited annual precipitation.

Tips and advice: Use structures
for shade, plant windbreaks,
choose plants that grow well in
this difficult environment, orient
your garden to give you a southern exposure for year-round outdoor enjoyment of a garden.

Rolling Plains
Texas Agricultural Extension
Service
District 3
Box 2159
Vernon, TX 76385-2159
940-552-9941

Wichita Falls

Average annual precipitation:
29 inches
Average last spring frost:
March 27
Average first fall frost:
November 11
Average growing season:
229 days
Horticulture Zone: 7

Mark Terning, Wichita Falls:
Wichita County Extension
Service
This area is in horticultural Zone
7a and 7b. Dry and hot summers
are typical. Winters can also be
extreme in some years.

Tips and advice: Protecting
your plants or transplants from
high winds in this area is critical.
Try using floating row crop covers on tomatoes and other plants.

North Texas
Texas Agricultural Extension
Service
District 4
17360 Coit Road
Dallas, TX 75252-6599
972-231-5362

Dallas

Average annual precipitation:
36 inches
Average last spring frost:
March 23
Average first fall frost:
November 13

Average growing season:
  235 days
Horticulture Zone: 7

Eva Estes, Keller: Rose Grower
We are in Zone 7 and our soil is
neutral to slightly alkaline. In
thirty-five years of moving and
establishing gardens, they have
all been in Zone 7, and that is
where the similarity ends. No
two soils are ever the same, and
all need some amendments.

  Tips and advice: Join a local
plant society. Read gardening
books for your particular area.
Realize the limitations of your
individual soils and climate, and
garden accordingly.

Rosa Finsley, Cedar Hill:
King's Creek Landscaping
In our particular area, we are fortunate because we are the dividing line between moist east Texas
and dry west Texas, and we can
grow a blend of species. It's an
exciting place to garden.

East Texas

Texas Agricultural Extension
  Service
District 5
P.O. Box 6
Overton, TX 75684
903-834-6191

Tyler
Average annual precipitation:

43 inches
Average last spring frost:
  March 7
Average first fall frost:
  November 21
Average growing season:
  259 days
Horticulture Zone: 8

Keith Hansen, Tyler: Smith
County Extension Service
The Tyler area could be considered one of the best locations in
Texas to be a gardener. We are
blessed with acidic soils that are
often very sandy; definite seasons; and an ability to grow a
wide palette of plants.

  One of the most important
things gardeners should do is to
have their soil tested for pH.
Because area soils are acidic—
some strongly so—many landscape and vegetable plants may
struggle if not suited to a low
pH.

  The definite change of seasons
allows us to take advantage of
plants with colorful fall foliage
and to grow many of the plants
that require a dormancy, brought
on by cold weather. However,
summers are hotter and more
humid than in other parts of the
southeast, putting stress on many
perennials and shrubs that won't
make it through the first year.

  Tips and advice: Be sure to
plant things at the right time.

For example, delay planting periwinkles until mid- to late May.
Then they will take off and grow
wonderfully well and be less
prone to fungal diseases that can
wipe out a bed of vinca, for
example.

Greg Grant, Nacogdoches:
Stephen F. Austin University
We have both heat and humidity,
and the combination is often
tough on plants, but we have
three good growing seasons—
spring, summer, and fall. During
summer we have tropical conditions. The rainfall is high,
between 45 and 60 inches annually, and we have high heat. But
in winter, it gets cold enough to
kill back tropical plants. It heats
up fast and cools down quickly.
The winds out of Canada come
straight down, causing temperatures to fluctuate dramatically.
Our soils are fairly acidic, usually
with a pH between 5.2 and 6.2.

Tips and advice: Face the facts:
This is not the northeastern U.S.
and you cannot grow lilacs,
astilbe, hosta, and peonies. It's
not fair to the plant or the gardener to put in a plant that
won't do well in your region.
Use plant material that will thrive
in our hot summers, such as
coleus, lantana, and fire bush.
Many of the Mediterranean
plants that would thrive in our
heat can't take the humidity.

Far West Texas
Texas Agricultural Extension
    Service
District 6
Box 1298
Ft. Stockton, TX 79735-1298
915-336-8585

El Paso
Average annual precipitation: less
    than 9 inches
Average last spring frost:
    March 9
Average first fall frost:
    November 12
Average growing season:
    248 days
Horticulture Zone: 8

Linda W. Rawe, Fort Stockton:
County Extension Service
Since water is the biggest
problem we have out here, I'd
strongly recommend the use of
mulch. Even inorganic mulches
are better than nothing. The soils
contain little organic matter, so
compost is a must. Iron deficiency is a problem, so the use of
chelated iron is a necessity.

The most important gardening point, however, is to select
appropriate plant material. It has
to be drought tolerant. The
evaporation rate is extremely
high, so providing a windbreak
from the southwesterly winds will
help. Keep turf to a minimum to
help reduce the amount of water
needed for the landscape.

West Central Texas

Texas Agricultural Extension
   Service
District 7
7887 U.S. Highway 87 North
San Angelo, TX 76901-9714
915-653-4576

Abilene
Average annual precipitation:
   25 inches
Average last spring frost:
   March 31
Average first fall frost:
   November 11
Average growing season:
   225 days
Horticulture Zone: 7

*John E. Begnaud, San Angelo:
Tom Green County Extension
Service*
The San Angelo area is a transi-
tional one where the rolling
plains, trans-Pecos, and Edwards
Plateau meet. Our elevation
ranges from 1,700 to 2,600 feet,
with predominantly clay loam
soil, ranging in depth from deep
to less than 10 inches on hillsides
and caliche outcroppings. Winters are dry with short cold
spells, and summer is unfailingly
hot.
   Tips and advice: Gardeners
must consider wind, water,
and soil types when planting,
and xeriscaping should be
utilized.

Central Texas

Texas Agricultural Extension
   Service
District 8
Route 2 Box 1
Stephenville, TX 76401
254-968-4145

Fort Worth
Average annual precipitation:
   31 inches
Average last spring frost:
   March 26
Average first fall frost:
   November 11
Average growing season:
   230 days
Horticulture Zone: 7

*Nancy Roe, Stephenville: Texas
A&M Research and Extension
Center*
In Central and North Central
Texas, you can garden almost all
year round. There are basically
three gardening seasons: spring,
summer, and fall. The frost-free
season is variable, but generally
lasts from March 14 to 20 to
November 15 to 20.
   Onions can be planted as early
as January, followed by cool season crops, which can be planted
through March. During late
March and early April, warm season plantings begin, and these
may continue into early July.
The fall cool-season crops, which
are planted in August and
September, may be harvested

through Thanksgiving or even Christmas.

Most of our soils are black clay, but there are also large areas with red clay or sandy soils. Because the black clay drains poorly, raised beds, which drain well, make the best gardening beds. All the native soils need the addition of organic matter. Compost is usually considered the best soil additive. Organic mulch, such as wood chips, bark, and hay, is also important as this helps moderate changes in soil temperatures and helps conserve moisture.

Tips and advice: Although annual rainfall totals may sound adequate for gardening, the rain distribution during the growing season is usually sporadic, which makes dry land gardening difficult. We recommend a low-volume method of irrigation, such as drip or trickle. This is the best way to ensure adequate moisture when needed. Irrigating in this way and using other innovations such as floating row covers to protect against cold and insects, when used correctly, can make gardening in Central Texas a little easier and more successful.

Southeast Texas
Texas Agricultural Extension
  Service

District 9
P.O. Box 2150
Bryan, TX 77806-2150
409-845-6800

Houston
Average annual precipitation:
  46 inches
Average last spring frost:
  February 14
Average first fall frost:
  December 11
Average growing season:
  300 days
Horticulture Zone: 9

Bill Adams and Tom LeRoy, Houston: Harris County Extension Service
Along the Gulf Coast, you have high humidity and high rainfall, up to 45 inches annually. South of Houston, there is less rainfall but still high humidity. What's really surprising about growing regions in Texas is how rapidly they change, particularly along the coast. Climatic changes occur every 10 miles when you're within 50 miles of the coast. In the eastern part of Harris County, you have sandy, acidic soils. On the southwest side of the county, you have clay soils.

Tips and advice: One of the tricks of gardening here is locating microclimates on your site and finding crops and plants that grow in these sites.

Garry McDonald, College Station: Texas A&M University
We are located in College Station in Central Texas in what is known as the post-oak savannah and blackland prairies. Our soils are heavy alkaline clays that drain poorly. The soils tend to be either sticky wet or brick hard.

Tips and advice: Use raised beds to improve drainage, amend the soil with organic matter, and use a prodigious amount of mulch to even out soil moisture. Select plant material carefully.

Southwest Texas

Texas Agricultural Extension
   Service
District 10
P.O. Box 1849
Uvalde, TX 78802-1849
830-278-9151

Uvalde
Average annual precipitation:
   24 1/2 inches
Average last spring frost:
   March 10
Average first fall frost:
   November 21
Average growing season:
   255 days
Horticulture Zone: 9

Jerry Parsons, San Antonio: Bexar County Extension Service
In San Antonio, the soil pH

ranges from 7.8 to 8.2 and vegetables seem to be ideally suited to these soils. We do have extreme fluctuations in temperature, and it can get cold very quickly. In San Antonio, the average first frost date is November 15 and the last is March 15. Within 40 miles of here, though, you move into a different planting zone. South, the last frost date is in February, but in the Hill Country, toward the north, it's in April.

Tips and advice: Use a frost row cover on vegetables when you plant early in spring. Water amply when going into a stressful period, either cold or hot. Prepare the soil well, adding organic matter. Use mulch when the soil temperature reaches 70°.

Coastal Bend

Texas Agricultural Extension
   Service
District 11
Route 2 Box 589
Corpus Christi TX 78406-9704
512-265-9203

Horticulturist
710 E. Main
Robstown, TX 78308
512-767-5217

Corpus Christi
Average annual precipitation: 30
   inches

Average last spring frost:
February 9
Average first fall frost: December
15
Average growing season: 309
days
Horticulture Zone: 9

Michael Womack, Robstown:
Nueces County Extension
Service
This area has both tropical and
semi-arid qualities, providing the
opportunity for growing a myriad of plants, from tropical hibiscus to prickly pear cactus.

Summer heat is intense with
temperatures approaching 100°,
high humidity, and bright, sunny
days. Winters are mild, with
most freezes occurring between
December 15 and February 15,
providing opportunities for a
long growing season. Average
rainfall in Nueces County is
about 36 inches, with heavy concentrations in October, March,
and April. It tends to be dry
from June through August.
Strong prevailing southeasterly
winds from the Gulf of Mexico
provide another gardening challenge in areas that lack trees to
break the wind.

Soils in the area vary dramatically. Along the coastline, the
soils are sandy, challenging gardeners not only with excessive
heat from the highly reflective
sand particles, but also with poor

water retention. Inland areas
have large concentrations of
heavy "gumbo" clay. These soils
drain poorly and during dry periods, the clay cracks and becomes
extremely hard and unworkable.

The key to successful gardening, for either soil type, is to garden in raised beds or to add large
amounts of organic matter to the
soil. Commonly used organic
matter includes compost, peat
moss, pine bark mulch, cotton
burr compost, manure, and grass
clippings. Sand needs additional
humus for water retention.
Humus breaks down quickly in
our warm, humid environment
and will need to be added to garden plots and flower beds once
or twice a year. Because of the
severe leaching, sandy soils also
need slow-release fertilizers that
contain nearly equal proportions
of nitrogen, phosphorous, and
potassium. These should be
applied three times a year, in
March, July, and October.

Adding organic matter to clay
soils helps break up the soil, thus
increasing both drainage and pli-
ability. Clay soils only need fertilizer twice a year, in spring and
fall. Because much of this land
was once farmland, the soil tends
to have high concentrations of
phosphorous. Fertilizers should
have a ratio of 3 to 4 parts nitrogen, 1 part phosphorous, and 1
to 2 parts potassium.

Tips and advice: The key to surviving the heat of summer is in increased shade and applying xeriscape principles. Selecting native and adapted water-wise plants and increasing shade should be the basis of any landscape. Early spring and fall bedding plants include snapdragons, petunias, marigolds, calendulas, alyssum, salvia, verbena, flowering cabbage and kale, begonias, impatiens, and pansies. Summer bedding plants include purslane, portulaca, and periwinkles (vinca).

The challenges are many but the rewards of gardening in this area are equally abundant.

South Texas

Texas Agricultural Extension
  Service
District 12
2401 East Highway 83
Weslaco, TX 78596
956-968-5581

McAllen
Average annual precipitation:
  23 1/2 inches
Average last spring frost:
  February 7
Average first fall frost:
  December 8
Average growing season:
  327 days
Horticulture Zone: 9

Julian Sauls, Weslaco: Texas A&M University Extension Service
Here, in the Rio Grande Valley, the climate is drier and warmer than in the citrus growing regions in Florida. The soils are alkaline to moderately alkaline, but we do little to adjust the pH. Good drainage is critical, particularly if you're growing citrus.

Tips and advice: Select your garden site carefully. Since our cold weather comes from the northwest, plant trees on the southeast side of the house and the structure itself will offer some protection.

Glyn Whiddon, Harlingen: Stuart Place Nursery
We are in a subtropical region. We usually have a few light freezes but usually no hard freezes. That allows us to use a wide range of tropical materials. Strong and frequent Gulf winds are also a factor. It is generally a lack of water, rather than the cold, that is the limiting factor.

Tips and advice: Use xeriscaping when planning your garden. You can have a nice mixture of plants that look tropical but have low water requirements.

ORGANIC AND HEIRLOOM GARDENS

HOWARD GARRETT
Dallas: The Natural Way

What's a former aspiring land-scape architect doing with his own radio show, a weekly news-paper column, and four published books? Only Howard Garrett, a.k.a. the "Dirt Doctor," can tell you: "The turning point came for me when my daughter, Logan, was born in 1985. This was when I committed my entire career to the research, education, and promotion of organic land-scaping, gardening, farming, ranching, and basic soil management."

And when Howard Garrett commits, he does it wholeheartedly. His enthusiastic belief in gardening "The Natural Way," as his radio show is called, has changed the way Texans have gardened. Through his dedicated efforts, information about organic gardening is easy to come by, and organic products now line the shelves in gardening centers in many regions of Texas.

How have you seen the interest in organic gardening change over the years?

In 1989 you could only find a few organic gardening products anywhere. Today, over twenty retail gardening stores in the Dallas/Ft. Worth area are 100 percent organic. They sell no toxic chemicals or artificial fertilizers. In addition, another eighty to one hundred stores have a separate department that offers a full line of organic products. What has happened here in this area has not happened anywhere else in the United States.

Carrots

It's interesting because we've only been "inorganic" since World War II. Prior to that everyone gardened organically. We had no choice since chemicals were not available to us. So, instead of being something new, organic gardening is really gardening like our ancestors did.

How do you define the term "organic"?

We try to take a commonsense approach to the definition of organic. To us, "organic" means understanding the primacy of organic matter and using products and techniques so that everything you do is beneficial to the soil. Some people say that anything that contains carbon is organic, but there are some really nasty things that contain carbon, including pesticides, such as diazinon.

If someone is in doubt as to whether or not to use a certain product, I tell them to ask themselves, "If I use this product, will it hurt or help the earthworms?" This is a simple way to decide what to buy. Our definition is not whether or not it contains carbon, but whether or not it is beneficial to the soil.

Is it possible to overuse organic products?

Of course. You can overuse anything, including water. It's important to know how to use even organic products. Some-

thing such as orange oil can do a lot of damage if it's used incorrectly. One of my octogenarian followers always overuses everything. If I suggest that she use one pound of something, she'll use twenty. For example, I told her to put some ground-up orange peel into the ground to help repel nematodes around her tomatoes. She called and said, "Howard, if you use too much of this stuff it will kill the earthworms!" So, just because it's organic does not mean that you can use it in unlimited quantities.

Are there commercial products available that help control insects in the garden?

Since 1989 we've been experimenting with organic tools to control insect pests. We are going to simpler and simpler biological products. Even organic products vary in how toxic they are. Orange oil will kill any insect, so we use it carefully and try to use the least toxic material available that will get the job done. We are trying to build the life in the soil—the earthworms and microorganisms. The secret to good gardening is a healthy root system, and that results in healthy plants that have a tremendous natural resistance to disease and insects. Healthy, adapted plants just won't have many problems.

Are most organic products readily available?

Yes, in our part of the state particularly. We're lucky in Texas to have Malcolm Beck in San Antonio. He was an organic farmer for twenty years before he decided to form a company called Gardenville, which produces organic gardening products. Now you can find his products all over the state. Not only are the products good, the instructions on the packages will tell you exactly how to use the material.

What are some of the basic organic products that every gardener should have on hand?

I recommend manure teas, which anyone can make, and citrus oil products. For insect control, I recommend natural diatomaceous earth. You can even feed this to pets and livestock because it helps control internal parasites and works as a natural nutrient supplement, providing trace minerals.

A concoction that I made up was named "Garrett Juice" by our listeners. It's made of manure compost tea, apple cider vinegar, liquid seaweed, and molasses. Gardenville makes it commercially but you can also make it up yourself. Our goal is not to make money off of organics, but to spread the word. It

GARRETT JUICE
1–2 cups manure-based compost tea
1 tablespoon molasses
1 tablespoon natural apple cider vinegar
1 tablespoon liquid seaweed

For added disease and insect control add:
1/4 cup garlic tea
1–2 oz. citrus oil

doesn't matter who came up with what. These are not secrets. All this comes from nature anyway so it belongs to everyone. We will tell you exactly what is in each product. There are many, many things you can make yourself but the American public is basically lazy and would rather buy a ready-made product rather than make it themselves. The lack of commercial products really held us back in the beginning.

How effective are organic methods in large, commercial projects?

The fastest growing portions of my radio audience are the farmers and ranchers. The reason is that these people have to worry about making a living from the land. The decisions they make about techniques and products affect their livelihoods. More and more, they are realizing that the traditional methods of fertilizing and spraying are expensive and are not working well. Once you can get them to try the organic approach, most of them are pleased with the results. Many of these people are very conservative folks who equated "organic" with "hippie." But money talks and what we are really all about is common sense and economics.

Many big, commercial land-scapes are also turning toward an organic approach. I designed the Frito Lay national headquarters, in Plano, Texas, which covers 300 acres and is totally organic. It is the largest completely organic landscape program in the world. It has been a great research project for us as well as a great client. We also converted the Johnson & Johnson Medical complex, a 100-acre site in Arlington, Texas, to organic. The first year we saved them fourteen thousand dollars by recycling organic matter, using less water, and mowing less frequently. It gets easier and less expensive each year.

How does a home owner get started in a basic organic program?

Some people are turned off to organic gardening because they think it is too confusing. But it's really all common sense. To begin with, we tell people to aer-ate the soil, then use compost

HOWARD GARRETT'S BASIC ORGANIC PROGRAM

• Select native or adapted plants.
• Aerate the soil.
• Build the organic content in the soil.
• Build the mineral content of the soil.
• Mulch with an organic material.
• Do not use poisons or any-thing that harms the microbes and insects—above and below the soil.
• Encourage biodiversity.

and compost-based fertilizer. We also recommend using volcanic rock. Anything that comes from volcanic activity helps produce highly productive soils. Lava holds the right level of moisture and has low levels of natural energy. We also recommend Texas greensand. These are read-ily available. Red lava sand from New Mexico, for example, is sold by the bag or the truckload. We've found that when a healthy balance of materials is found in the soil, pH will move to the correct level.

We tell people to watch nature and imitate what goes on in the natural world. For example, in the forest, the trees mulch underneath every time they drop leaves and needles.

Every year in an organic program, the beds should get better and better. Building the soil is an ongoing process. The easiest thing to control with organics is disease because with healthy soils, disease problems essentially go away.

Do you recommend using native plants?

A plant has to be adapted to the area where it is planted, otherwise it doesn't matter what the gardener does. Native plants are great, but many introduced plants are good too. If you only used native plants in Texas, you wouldn't have any food. In some parts of the country, you have to use imported plants that can adapt to your particular situation.

An organic program helps the adaptability of the plants. We've actually increased the freeze tolerance of plants by using organics. We don't have as many pest and disease problems, we don't

---

THE NATURAL WAY TIPS

- **Test the soil** to determine available levels of organic matter and minerals.
- **Based on the results of your test, add organic matter as needed.** The Texas Plant and Soil lab (956-383-0739) in Edinburg offers organic recommendations.
- **Prepare beds by adding compost** (4–5 inches), lava sand (40–80 pounds), organic fertilizer (20 pounds) and sugar (5 pounds) per 1,000 square feet of bed. Till into the native soil at a depth of 3 inches.
- **Apply organic fertilizer** two or three times a year. During the growing season, spray turf, tree and shrub foliage, trunks, limbs, and soil each month with compost tea or Garrett Juice. **Add lava sand** annually at 40–80 pounds/1,000 square feet.
- **Mulch 1–3 inches** around shrubs and trees. Mulch vegetable gardens with 8 inches of alfalfa hay, rough-textured compost, or shredded native tree trimmings.
- **Adjust watering schedule** to allow for deep, infrequent waterings to maintain an even moisture level.
- **Mow weekly** to a height of 2 1/2 inches or taller and leave the clippings on the lawn to return nutrients and organic matter to the soil. Use a mulching mower if the budget allows.

have to water as much or replant as often.

Do you recommend using cover crops?

We tell everyone—from home owners to farmers and ranchers—that you never want bare soil. You can use an organic mulch or grow cover crops, but do something to cover up the bare soil. There are many good cover crops to use, such as vetches, clover, or barley. In the orchards, you want native grasses to grow. Whatever you use, be careful not to let it get tall enough to compete with the crops. When you cut, don't mow all at one time, so that you will leave a nursery for the beneficial insects. Everything you do should be aimed toward stimulating life.

Traditionally, many annuals and bedding plants seem to need a lot of fertilizer. How do you handle this?

We suggest that people use manure tea, but even that might make weak cells in plants. We really emphasize feeding the soil and not the plants.

Are there resource materials that you recommend?

Bargyla Rateaver, a professor at University of California at Riverside, wrote some wonderful books and has set up a total organic curriculum at the school. She has debunked one of the major myths about how plants take up nutrients and wrote a book about it. We were all taught that plants only take up nutrients as basic elements or ions and the entire synthetic approach to gardening is based on that. The common belief was that the plant can't tell the difference between an organic and an inorganic fertilizer. She proves this wrong and explains in great detail that plants can absorb big chunks of matter. Water is a molecule, not an ion, and plants will suck it right up. Roots can absorb an entire bacteria. But that's not what has been taught all these years, and it takes time for people to accept this.

I also recommend *ACRES USA*, a newspaper dedicated to organic gardening.

Do you have any other advice?

If you haven't rid yourself of toxic chemicals yet, go ahead and do it right now. Go 100 percent organic.

For more information, look for Howard Garrett's column, "The Natural Way," in the *Dallas Morning News* Friday House and Garden section or his Web site: <www.wbap.com> or <dirt-doctor.com>. E-mail: groundcrew@yahoo.com.

WILLIAM C. WELCH
College Station: Texas A&M University

Well known to gardeners in Texas and throughout the South-eastern United States, William C. Welch has enjoyed a long and fruitful career in horticulture. A Houston native, William attended Louisiana State University, where he received a degree in landscape architecture and earned both his master's and doctoral degrees in extension education and horticulture. In 1972, he joined the staff of Texas A&M, where he still serves as extension landscape horticulturist.

In addition to working with professional growers, garden and civic groups, and an increasingly enthusiastic gardening public, William finds time to write extension service publications, magazine articles, and popular books such as *Perennial Garden Color, Antique Roses for the South*, and *The Southern Heirloom Garden*.

Although anything green and growing seems to capture his attention, William's current horticultural passions include native plants, old garden roses, perennials, historic gardening, and southern cottage gardening.

What is heirloom gardening?

It is utilizing plants and garden ideas that have stood the test of time. An heirloom garden and a cottage garden could be the same thing, depending on the design and the selection of plant material. A cottage garden is usually small, has no lawn and is enclosed by a fence, walls, or hedges. An heirloom garden may or may not contain these same elements.

Although it's fun and challenging to rebuild an heirloom garden using the bones of an original old garden, it's not absolutely necessary to do it this way. You can create an heirloom garden from scratch.

What are some of the historic influences on Texas gardens?

Texans have been influenced by many different cultures including German, French, Native American, African American, Spanish, and English. Although immigrants from these countries and the Native Americans could not transplant their childhood

Crinum lily

gardens intact, they could interpret those influences in some way and create a new garden with their ideas and memories.

When you look at a garden and want to determine what influenced it, what do you look for?

One of the first things to look for are some of the hardscapes in the garden, elements such as fences, walls, and walks. Then look at the kind of plant material used and how it is used. For example, is it a formal landscape? Does it include a lot of color?

What are some of the elements that indicate a French influence?

The most obvious is the use of *parterres* (hedges trimmed to form a series of geometric patterns) and an overall formal design, although there was also usually unity or balance between the dwelling and the garden. The French liked to dominate nature and used a lot of trimmed trees and shrubs in their gardens, often planted in long *allées*. They also used an abundance of color and fragrance from flowers, vegetables, and herbs, and accessories such as bell jar cloches. Outbuildings in French gardens included structures such as *pigeonerres* (similar to dovecotes). Other influences would include the abundant use of plants in containers and a separation between the pleasure and utilitarian areas.

What influence did African Americans have on gardening in the South?

One of the most important is that they had the good judgment to hold on to a lot of plants, whether they were plants that they brought with them from Africa, or plants that they were given, or ones that they found when they arrived here. For example, some of the finest old roses in Texas are found in the gardens of African Americans. This might have been because they did not have resources to buy new plants, or it could be that they were able to appreciate the beauty of some of the plants they already had—probably a combination of the two. But I think there is a real lesson to be learned here. They loved, and used, a lot of flamboyant color in their gardens and introduced plants such as okra, yams, and some crinums.

The African Americans, like several other cultures, used the garden very much like a living room, where they had outdoor kitchens and living spaces. The flower garden was generally found in the front yard, and all the yards were highly decorated with art objects. The yards themselves were usually swept clean with a broom.

Richard Westmacott has written a very good book on the subject entitled *African-American Gardens and Yards in the Rural South*.

What elements indicate a Spanish influence?

You can see this most dramatically in the open plazas of the towns and cities. Both civic and home gardens were often planted on a four-part design with a central water feature. In Spanish gardens, you'll often find a formal, symmetrical design in contrast with a more informal, asymmetrical design. Although many of the gardens were very small, they were planted carefully and intensely.

The Spanish used bold colors in their choice of garden flowers and these contrasted beautifully with the earth-toned backgrounds. Many of these gardens were enclosed with walls that were decorated, along with various water features, with painted tiles.

What about the German influence?

Texas has been influenced by Germany probably more than any other state has. The Germans brought some very good botanists here, men such as Ferdinand Lindheimer, who

> ## GERMAN GARDEN INFLUENCES
>
> - Generous use of fruits and vegetables.
> - Neat and orderly gardens.
> - Summer houses for enjoying the outdoors.
> - Rows of cut flowers in vegetable gardens.
> - High value on trees for shade and ornament.

found dozens of plants in the wild that he then sent to Harvard and the Missouri Botanical Gardens in the 1840s.

The Germans were very methodical and tended to be neat and orderly. They expected everyone else to be that way too. Germans did particularly well with fruits and vegetables. The Moravians, who are Germans, moved to North Carolina and built the town of Salem and did some interesting things in gardening. They planted vegetables on diagonals and built summer houses for sitting and enjoying the outdoors. They also planted rows of cut flowers in the vegetable gardens for use in the house and grew lots of roses, which they passed down from one generation to the next. The Germans placed a high value on trees for shade and ornament and used them not only close to their homes, but also to line the town streets.

The excellent craftsmanship of these people showed up in the stone, wood, and iron work in the landscape.

What about the English?

During the Victorian era, people such as William Robinson and Gertrude Jekyll held a naturalistic approach to gardening, meaning that they used ornamental plants in naturalized settings. Others in England during this time period used "bedding out," the use of an abundance of flowering material in set designs. It was a highly refined and formal kind of gardening that Gertrude Jekyll did not appreciate at all.

In spite of this, Jekyll's landscape designs had a high degree of structure. She had a unique style of using plants in drifts,

---

GERTRUDE JEKYLL
GARDEN INFLUENCES

• Ornamental plants in a naturalized setting.
• Planting in drifts, cottage style.
• Hand-me-down or heirloom varieties.
• High degree of structure in the garden.

---

similar to the cottage garden style. She obtained many of her plants from the cottagers, whom she considered to be the best source of plant material. Some of these plants were hand-me-downs, some were native.

The British influence has been obvious is some high-profile American gardens, such as Williamsburg. How has the garden restoration philosophy changed there in the past ten years?

Williamsburg is now called a Colonial Revival Garden. The state of the art of garden restoration was different in the 1920s, when Williamsburg was built, than it is today. Much of what was done in Williamsburg is being criticized now because all the gardens look so much alike. Arthur Shurwood, the original landscape architect for Colonial Williamsburg, designed it this way. For example, according to his original landscape design, all of the fences were painted white and most of the beds were in geometric shapes, providing little variation from one garden to the next.

Today, we know that that is not what these early Williamsburg gardens really looked like. But the reality is that Williamsburg is a very public landscape and, being so, must present a sense of beauty and maintenance. They have to juggle both painting a pretty picture and doing something authentic.

Landscape historians are also currently conducting cutting-edge research at Carter's Grove Plantation and other sites along the James River and doing a great job of interpreting their findings.

There seem to be many highly talented people in the field of garden restoration. Who are they and what are they working on?

Two of the best are Peter Hatch and Peggy Newcomb at Monticello, as well as Dean Norton at Mount Vernon. Both Jefferson and Washington were enthusiastic gardeners and the horticultural legacy they left is exciting. Monticello, in particular, has wonderful resources. Jefferson's mind for gardening, as for nearly everything else, was just fabulous and he documented everything very well.

For someone fortunate enough to have an old garden, are there guidelines for restoring it? How do you go about doing a garden reconstruction?

The first thing I would advise is to get Rudy Fevretti's excellent book, *For Every House, A Garden, A Guide for Reproducing Period Gardens.*

After that, do some research of your own. Find out if there was anything written—records, nursery orders, letters, and such. And then research what was growing there during that time period. Look at old nursery catalogs to get some idea. These are available many places. In Texas, they are on file at the Center for American History at the University of Texas in Austin. Or you can pull them up on the Internet through the National Agricultural Library.

Once you've done some basic research, you should decide on a garden style, based on the architecture of the house and what you can determine about the original garden. Is it formal or informal? If it was originally a formal garden, what were the ethnic influences? Were the original owners French? British?

If it is an informal style, it's a little easier to reconstruct. One of the reasons that cottage gardens are so popular now is because it was a style prevalent in the South for so many years. Today, just as in earlier days, people liked this style because it is so flexible and allows for individual expression. Cottage gardens can include herbs, perennials, roses, and other flowering shrubs. They are relatively easy to design and maintain and can be fairly

GUIDELINES FOR
RESTORING AN
HEIRLOOM GARDEN

- Find out as much as you can about your individual garden—look for records, nursery orders, letters, etc.
- Research the time period—read books, look at old nursery catalogs.
- Decide on a garden style based on the architecture of the house and what you can determine about the original garden.
- Select plants and a style authentic to the time period.

authentic to a time period with the careful selection of plants.

What are some of your favorite heirloom plants?

It's hard to narrow it down, but I love antique roses, mock orange, flowering quince, pomegranates, phlox, narcissus, and crinums, just to name a very few.

LIBBIE WINSTON
Navasota: The Peaceable Kingdom

If there ever was a flesh and blood Earth Mother, it has to be Libbie Winston. Founder and director of The Peaceable Kingdom, a Central Texas school dedicated to teaching about organic gardening and crafts, Libbie has both a degree in psychology and an unshakable faith in the goodness of the land.

When she moved to her Texas farm in 1970, the land had been badly overgrazed. "We were in the middle of a drought and the soil looked as if it wouldn't grow much of anything," Libbie remembers. "But I got on an old Ford tractor, threw fifty-pound bags of vetch and rye seed over my shoulder, and began to work the soil until things began to come back." So successful were her efforts that soon local ranchers were coming by to marvel at the recovery of the land.

Libbie's organic approach to gardening and farming was unusual in Texas at that time. "Many people thought I was a little crazy," she admits, "but a lot of people were curious and wanted to learn how to do it themselves. They would come for a day, and then some started bringing sleeping bags and staying all night, and after a year or two, we decided to make it an official school, since that's essentially what it was anyway."

The charter for the school was broad and included the teaching of arts, crafts, and related disciplines. Many craftsmen came to teach a variety of skills—all of which centered around the land.

Potters made glazes from the native clays, blacksmiths made garden gates, weavers used natural dyes. The biggest emphasis was on herbs, however, and chefs from Houston quickly realized the value of locally grown herbs.

The school, chartered in 1971, officially closed in 1997, but the classes and workshops held during that time touched

Calendula

many lives. One of the last programs of the school was growing heirloom and open-pollinated plants. Libbie worked closely with the national Seed Saver's Exchange in Decorah, Iowa, an organization dedicated to saving old and rare types of seed from extinction, and with Seeds of Change, a seed company that promotes the use of organically grown heirloom seeds.

What is the difference between a hybrid variety and an open-pollinated variety?

A hybrid is the result of inter-breeding between two or more species, races, or varieties. Most patented hybrids do not breed true from seed or are sterile. If you try to grow them out, traits from one or another of the parents will emerge, producing an often undesirable plant. Modern hybrid vegetables are bred for reasons other than taste and nutrition. Today, characteristics such as good shipping, yield, ease of mechanized harvest, and long-keeping traits are important in commercially grown plants. In nature, hybrids occur and may stabilize after a number of generations to create new species or invigorate old ones. Open-pollinated plants, on the other hand, breed true to the parent plant.

What happens if you collect seed from a hybrid and replant it?

It is illegal to collect and replant seed from a patented hybrid plant. Anyway, the seed would be sterile, or revert to its inbred forebears.

Why is using open-pollinated varieties important?

First and foremost, you do not have to buy open-pollinated seed every year if you wish to save your own seed. In countries such as India and Kenya, open-pollinated seed may be the difference between having food and starving. Hybrid seed crops require more off-farm inputs, such as chemical fertilizers and pesticides. In developing countries, most farmers cannot afford to buy seeds and chemicals every year. Planting hybrid plants means that they cannot be self-sufficient.

Every society must be concerned about the loss of diversity in our gene pool. The scientists who create hybrids must be concerned because they draw on a repository of open-pollinated genetic choices. Since 1902, 80 percent of the vegetable varieties available in the U.S. have been lost.

The Vavilov Institute in St. Petersburg (Leningrad) had, at the beginning of World War II, a 180,000-accession collection of seeds and plant material from around the world. In 1942, the scientists and staff who protected the collection died of starvation at their desks, surrounded by rice and other seeds. They knew that preserving this collection of the genetic material found in these seeds was more important than their own lives.

What are the advantages of using open-pollinated varieties?

The genetic variability found within open-pollinated seeds may provide resistance to pests or

diseases that would otherwise wipe out a hybrid monoculture.

Plants that have been grown in the same type of climate and soil for a number of years become acclimated and are best suited to growing in that particular type of area.

The most important thing about organic gardening is feeding the soil. If you get the soil right, the plants will take care of themselves. Organic gardening is not a quick fix. When you follow nature's rhythm, you do less work and nature does more. Start with the firm foundation of healthy soil and much less effort will be involved in the long run.

Are all heirloom varieties open-pollinated?

No. The most famous heirloom hybrids are roses. Unless a rose is a wild or species rose, it must be propagated vegetatively, usually by cuttings. During the Napoleonic Wars, the Empress Josephine requested that her husband collect roses from around the world, and she grew them in her garden at Malmaison, thereby preserving many hybrid heirlooms for

OPEN-POLLINATED VEGETABLES AND HERBS SUITED FOR TEXAS

Cherokee Trail of Tears beans—purple foliage and black beans, planted to grow up corn stalks. Produces well in light shade. This variety was planted along the Trail of Tears, the route taken by the Cherokee tribe when they were driven out of North Carolina to Oklahoma.

Texas Shoepeg corn—drought tolerant Texas heirloom with notable disease and insect resistance. Produces two or three fat yellow ears whose oddly shaped, pointed kernels are good both fresh, when young, and dried and ground for corn meal.

Louisiana Long Green eggplant—very heat tolerant, thin-skinned mild eggplant. Grill it with olive oil, or roast it with pesto. You don't even need to peel this one—eat it hide, hair, and feathers.

Zeigler's Heirloom Bibb lettuce—brought to Texas from Germany in the last century by the Zeigler family of Bryan. Both winter hardy and slow to bolt with the heat. Beautiful light green, it has acclimatized to our area, producing when no other lettuce does.

Texas Wild tomato—in a class all its own, bush is huge and sprawling, fruit tiny. Flavor is the essence of tomato. Prolific producer, right through heat of summer into fall.

Enrico Ray arugula—delicious, slow-to-bolt variety, brought to Texas by an Italian immigrant, preserved by his grandson in Brenham, Texas. Makes a delectable pesto, though not for the faint of heart. Use the seeds for sprouting, or grind them as a mustard substitute.

Hill Country Red okra—beautiful, tasty summer producer, reseeds readily.

Chiltepin pepper—blindingly hot perennial with small fruit and delicate leaves. Useful as an ornamental in the flowerbed, good to flavor vinegar. (**Bird Pepper**, another name for chiltepin, is a native of Texas and Mexico. Ours comes from a ranch in Sabinal.)

Purple tomatillo—not only makes traditional salsa verde, but is sweet eaten out of hand. Naturalized easily and grows through the hottest summer.

Devil's Claw—fibrous seed pods were used by Hohokam Indians in basketry. Also used in crafts and arrangements; young pods are edible.

OPEN-POLLINATED FLOWERS SUITED FOR TEXAS

Hens-and-Chicks calendula—old type whose flowers send out tiny florets from behind the petals in a sprightly encore. Petals are edible and medicinal. Will reseed and grow in high shade.

Old-fashioned petunia—stable, natural hybrid, blooms profusely in sun or light shade, makes a spreading bush that climbs to 6 feet with support, reseeds readily. Evening scented and makes a long-lasting cut flower. Grows in dooryard gardens throughout the South, although plants and seeds are rarely available commercially.

Cresta de Gallo—tall red cockscomb with a huge, deep red head. Loves the summer heat, dries well, and naturalizes. Our plant originally came from a swept garden in Mesilla, New Mexico.

Gulf Coast penstemon—native Texas perennial about 30 inches tall with luminous purple flowers; blooms for a long period in the spring. Grows either on dry or poorly drained ground, reseeds freely.

posterity. If you, as I do, have a rose such as 'Souvenir de la Malmaison', it must have come originally from Josephine's garden via cuttings. Imagine the history of these plants as they are passed from hand to hand over the centuries.

If you're planting perennial plants, such as rosemary, is it still important to use an old-fashioned variety or could you include one of the varieties that have been developed to be more cold hardy, for example?

Hardy rosemarys, such as 'Arp' or 'Hill Hardy', are great examples of natural selection. 'Arp' was found on the northern edge of its range, propagated by cuttings, and sent to the East Coast for trials. After a particularly hard winter, several plants survived to become the stock for 'Hill Hardy'. Plant breeders make the same kind of selections that nature does, by choosing desirable traits.

Sentiment often plays a part in seed and plant saving. Everyone wants the "flower that Grandma grew." One day I was driving down the street in a small town and saw a peculiar-looking rosemary. I stopped, knocked on the door, and asked to see it. On closer inspection, I could tell that branches from a big central plant had been bent down over pots full of soil, weighted with a rock and left to root. Once rooted, the branches were cut off the mother plant and put into the ground beside it. Over the years, the gardener had created quite a respectable rosemary hedge. When I asked her why she did it, she said that her Italian father had always grown it that way, and so she did too.

How do you collect seeds to replant?

Seed collection can be as simple or complicated as you want to make it. Simple rules are to collect ripe seeds on a dry day, sift the bugs and leaves out of them, set them on a plate inside for a couple of days to dry completely and to allow the insects to leave for greener shores, then put them in an airtight container and store in a cool, dark place. Then plant them as you would any other seed.

Can you collect seed from wildflowers or native plants to replant in your garden? Are there precautions you should follow?

Collecting seeds from native plants is a good idea, and is sometimes the only way to get them for your garden. Please be aware, though, that plant populations can be fragile. Collect

only if you see a large number of plants and remember that seeds are important for wildlife food as well as for the survival of a plant species. If you need large quantities, purchase them from a reputable wildflower grower.

Spiritually, a garden is the embodiment of the great cycle of birth, life, death, and rebirth celebrated in the world's great religions. And so, we have food for the soul.

Do you think organic gardening is simply a passing fad?

Organic gardening and farming is here to stay. Public demand here and in countries around the world will see to it. Health is a major concern and is the basis for one of the fastest growing industries in the United States. Senior citizens and parents of young children are equally interested in a healthy, high-quality food supply. Big grocery chains and canning companies are catering to their interest.

Environmentalism is a positive, moral concept that is not going to go away. People are becoming aware that you can have a glowing garden without using chemicals.

What is the most important thing about gardening organically?

Feeding the soil. If you get the soil right, the plants will take care of themselves. We cannot control nature and make it do whatever we want; the natural system is too subtle and complex for that. Slow down and observe. Organic gardening is not a quick fix. When you follow nature's rhythm, you do less work and nature does more. Start with the firm foundation of healthy soil and you'll expend much less energy in the long run.

What can we do to encourage wise land use in our own country?

Demand organically grown food. Recycle. Compost. Grow open-pollinated plants. Educate children. Educate legislators. Get involved. Most of all, take time for yourself to enjoy nature. Take a walk and just look at things. See how plants change each day. If you know an interested child, learn from him or her. Children are intensely observant.

Why are you so interested in gardening?

Gardening and plants are satisfying on every level. Intellectually, the sophistication and complexity of nature provides an unending source of food for thought. Physically, there is, of course, exercise and the satisfaction of growing your own delicious, healthy food for the body. Aesthetically, the scents, tastes, feel, form, color, and even sounds of a happy garden are a joy. Spiritually, a garden is the embodiment of the great cycle of birth, life, death and rebirth celebrated in the world's great religions. And so, we have food for the soul.

Resources

Sources of Seeds and Plants

Abundant Life Seed Foundation
P.O. Box 772
Port Townsend, WA 98368
360-385-5660

W. Atlee Burpee and Company
300 Park Avenue
Warminster, PA 18974

Erth Products
402 Line Creek Drive
Peachtree City, GA 30269
1-800-849-ERTH

Chemical-free fertilizer and soil conditioners

Flower and Herb Exchange
3076 North Winn Road
Decorah, IA 52101
319-382-5990

Nichol's Garden Nursery
1190 North Pacific Highway
Albany, OR 97321
541-928-9280

Old House Gardens
536 Third Street
Ann Arbor, MI 48103-4957
Source of antique bulbs

Park Seed
1 Parkton Avenue
Greenwood, SC 29647-0001
800-845-3369

Peaceful Valley Farm Supply
P.O. Box 2209
Grass Valley, CA 95945
916-272-4769
Organic growing supplies

Pinetree Garden Seeds
Box 300
New Gloucester, ME 04260
207-926-3400

Planet Natural
P.O. Box 3146
1612 Gold Avenue
Bozeman, MT 59772-3146

Seed Saver's Exchange
3076 North Winn Road
Decorah, IA 52101

Seeds of Change
P.O. Box 15700
Santa Fe, NM 88750-5700
800-957-2227

Select Seeds–Antique Flowers
180 Stickney Road
Union, CT 06076
860-684-9310

Shepherd's Garden Seed
30 Irene Street
Torrington, CT 06790-6627
203-482-3638

Thomas Jefferson Center for
    Historic Plants
Monticello
P.O. Box 316
Charlottesville, VA 22902
804-984-9816

Organizations

Historic Preservation Committee
American Society of Landscape
    Architects
636 I Street NW
Washington, D.C. 20001-3736

The Garden Conservancy
P.O. Box 219
Cold Spring, NY 10516
914-265-2029

Seed Saver's Exchange
3076 North Winn Road
Decorah, IA 52101

The Seeds of Texas Seed
    Exchange
P.O. Box 9882
College Station, TX 77842

Southern Garden History Society
Drawer F
Salem Station
Winston-Salem, NC 27108

Libraries

Cherokee Garden Library
Atlanta History Center
West Andrews Drive
Atlanta, GA

University of Texas
Life Science Library
Austin, TX
512-495-4630

Publications

BOOKS

Ashworth, Suzanne. *Seed to Seed.* Decorah, IA: Seed Saver Publications, 1995.

Donlan, Peter. *Growing to Seed.* Willits, CA: Ecology Action.

Druitt, Liz. *The Organic Rose Garden.* Dallas, TX: Taylor Publishing, 1996.

Druitt, Liz and Michael Shoup. *Landscaping with Antique Roses.* Newtown, CT: Taunton Press, 1992.

Favretti, Rudy. *For Every House A Garden, A Guide for Reproducing Period Gardens.* Chester, CT: Pequot Press, 1977.

———. *Landscapes and Gardens for Historic Buildings, American Association for State and Local History.* Walnut Creek, CA: AltaMira Press, 1991.

Garrett, Howard. *The Dirt Doctor's Guide to Organic Gardening.* Austin, TX: University of Texas Press, 1995.

———. *Howard Garrett's Organic Manual.* Fort Worth, TX: Summit Publishing, 1997.

———. *Howard Garrett's Texas Organic Gardening Book.* Houston, TX: Gulf Publishing Company, 1993.

———. *Plants of the Metroplex.* Austin, TX: University of Texas Press, 1998.

Martin, Laura. *Grandma's Garden.* Atlanta, GA: Longstreet Press, 1990.

Rodale's Successful Organic Gardening: Vegetables. Emmaus, PA: Rodale Press, 1993.

Rogers, Marc. *Saving Seeds: The Gardener's Guide to Growing and Storing Vegetable and Flower Seed.* Pownal, VT: Storey Communications, Inc., 1990.

Welch, William. *Antique Roses for the South.* Dallas, TX: Taylor Publishing Company, 1990.

Welch, William and Greg Grant. *The Southern Heirloom Garden.* Dallas, TX: Taylor Publishing Company, 1995.

Westmacott, Richard. *African-American Gardens and Yards in the Rural South.* Knoxville, TN: University of Tennessee Press, 1992.

MAGAZINES

Organic Gardening
Rodale Press
33 E. Minor Street
Emmaus, PA 18098

DESIGN

JAMES HARRIS
Lubbock: Landscape Architect

James Harris' interests encompass not only planting gardens and landscapes, but also educating people about wise land use practices. He holds a master's degree in landscape architecture from Louisiana State University but has lived in West Texas since 1975. His talents and expertise can be seen throughout the High Plains region of Texas, as he and his firm have been instrumental in landscape planning and design for projects such as the Amarillo Botanical Gardens, the University Medical Center at Texas Tech University in Lubbock, and other commercial, as well as residential, projects.

In addition, James has been an associate professor of landscape architecture at Texas Tech and has served on the Parks Board for the city of Lubbock. He has also served on many community boards, and was instrumental in introducing community gardening to the city of Lubbock.

"I am a landscape architect by profession," James says, "and a gardener by avocation. I grew up with a love of gardening that I learned from my grandparents, with whom I lived. And I've now carried that forward for about forty years."

How is designing a garden different in West Texas than it would be in other parts of the state?

Daisy chrysanthemum

We have a difficult gardening climate here. We get extreme temperatures and quick changes in the weather. The weather can be quite dramatic, particularly in spring. The old saying is, "If you don't like the weather, just stick around a few hours and it will change."

Lubbock is in USDA horticultural Zone 7a. Amarillo is in 6. Here in Lubbock, it goes down to 10° about once a year. It's actually not how cold it gets when you're selecting plants, but how fast it gets cold. For example, in November 1993, it was 70° one day and that night a blue norther moved in and the temperatures dropped to 7°. We had not had any previous freezes that would have hardened off plant material and sent them into dormancy, and as a result, that early hard freeze killed much of our plant material. It even froze out English ivy that had been here for a long time. The landscape literally turned black. Because something like this happens so quickly, all you can do to guard against losing plants is to mulch and water heavily before the weather turns.

In planning a garden here, you need to consider not only temperature extremes, but also elements such as prevailing winds, light intensity, light reflec-

tion, heat retention in hard surfaces close to garden beds, low humidity, high soil pH, soil texture, the high mineral content of the domestic water supply, and only 17 to 20 inches of precipitation annually.

The overall design of a landscape needs to go beyond cosmetics and consider these environmental elements as well.

In West Texas, the overall design of a landscape needs to go beyond cosmetics to consider environmental elements such as prevailing winds, light intensity, light reflection, heat retention, low humidity, high soil pH, soil texture, and the high mineral content of the domestic water supply.

For example, you might use structures for shade, use a row of trees or shrubs as a windbreak, or introduce a water feature that would add humidity and the sound of running water.

Water is a critical gardening issue here, and before you begin planning a landscape, there are several questions that need to be answered. Are you going to depend on natural rainfall or will you install an irrigation system for supplemental watering? If you do use an irrigation system, will the water supply originate from wells in the Ogalalla aquifer or from Lake Meredith, or a combination of both? The water from the lake has a high sodium content that contributes to poor soil structure and may even cause leaf burn in a number of plants. Well water that draws from the Ogalalla aquifer is hard water and contains calcium, manganese, and fluoride.

How do you make the best of the conditions you have?

You begin, if possible, with the most favorable orientation for your house or structure. Then analyze the property spaces around the building, taking into consideration orientation, sun and wind impact, drainage, and opportunities for collecting water from the roof and hardscape surfaces.

A southern exposure is best for year-round outdoor enjoyment of a garden. The next best is an eastern exposure. The west and north exposures are less desirable. The west side is impacted by prevailing spring winds and hot afternoon summer sun. The north is subject to cold-front winds and long shadows cast by a structure during winter.

From February to June we get strong winds from the west.

We're famous for our spring dust storms. This material comes from agricultural lands and during severe wind conditions, we'll get material from as far away as Arizona and New Mexico.

As domestic water prices continue to rise, it becomes more and more important to choose drought-resistant plants.

From late August through March we get frontal systems from the north-northwest to the south-southeast. Locals say that there's nothing between Lubbock, Texas, and the North Pole except barbed wire fence. The changes in temperature can be sudden and dramatic. If you can put in your garden so that it faces south and receives some buffer from the weather from the house, it will help.

How large a windbreak do you generally need and what kind of plant material do you use for this?

The rule of thumb is that a windbreak's influence along the ground is about 2 1/2 times its height. For example, if the mature height of the trees in your break is 30 feet, it will impact an area about 75 feet laterally downwind.

The most effective wind breaks use a combination of evergreen and deciduous trees and shrubs of varying heights. Not only does this look better than a single row of trees, it is also more effective. This allows some airflow to filter through the plantings. If you use a solid row of trees or something such as a fence or building, the air goes over the structure with increased airspeed and the downwind turbulence on the lee side is increased.

In an urban environment, the choice of plant material will be influenced by the proximity of plantings on neighboring properties. Where supplemental watering is available, the following plant material is appropriate: Eastern red cedar (*Juniperus virginiana*), Austrian pine (*Pinus nigra*), little leaf elm (*Ulmus parvifolia* var. *sempervirens*), cedar elm (*Ulmus crassifolia*), Elaeagnus (*Elaeagnus pungens*), photinia (*Photinia serrulata*), and yaupon holly (*Ilex vomitoria*).

In an unirrigated situation, consider desert pine (*Pinus elderica*), piñon pine (*Pinus cembroides* and *P. edulis*), one-seed juniper (*Juniperus monosperma*), Siberian elm (*Ulmus pumila*), Osage orange (*Maclura pomifera*), desert olive (*Forestiera neomexicana*), Spanish broom (*Spartium junceum*), Russian olive (*Elaeagnus angustifolia*), and rabbit brush (*Crysothamnus nauseosus*).

How far apart do you space these when you first plant?

Plan the windbreak planting with permanent, long-lived plant material spaced for mature growth. Then, fill in the spaces with temporary, short-lived plants that will succumb to crowding and competition. As the windbreak matures, remove the smaller plants, giving the permanent trees plenty of room to grow.

How about light requirements for plants in this area?

We have very bright light here because it's rarely cloudy and we have no haze resulting from air pollution or high ambient humidity. When plant catalogs talk about plants needing "full sun," here they need only about 4 to 6 hours of sunlight a day. Our introduced plants almost always benefit from shelter from the hot afternoon sun. Unfortunately, the kind of shade we have is dry shade, which is the most difficult kind of growing environment.

What are the soils like in this area?

Typically, around Lubbock, we have fine, sandy loam topsoil, which becomes more sandy in the counties west of here. Under the sandy loam is caliche (calcium carbonate). Toward Amarillo, the soils gradually have a higher and higher clay content, which makes difficult gardening soil.

If you want to grow plants that won't tolerate our alkaline soils, grow them in containers and irrigate with captured rain water or water that you've collected from air conditioner condensate.

The sandy loam soils have an excellent texture for growing plants, but are very alkaline. It's impractical to try to change the pH because we irrigate with water that is also alkaline. You can put iron and aluminum sulfates on the lawn, but every time you irrigate, you're reversing the process. Personally, I try to use plants that will tolerate a pH of 8.0 and above.

If you want to include a plant that won't tolerate alkaline soils, grow it in a container. That way, you'll have complete control. Container gardening is catching on in popularity here for that reason, and the amount of plant material available for containers is increasing dramatically.

Do you encourage people to compost?

It depends on the person. If you're an avid gardener, it will be worth your while. Composting is difficult here. Because it is so dry, the material doesn't decompose very quickly. It takes a lot of effort to keep the compost material moist enough to decompose.

How do you go about choosing plants for a garden in this area?

The first thing people need to learn if they have moved here from a different region is that they must change the way they garden. You can't transplant gardening thoughts from back East or the Northeast or wherever else you're from because gardening here is completely different.

The hardest thing for people to become accustomed to is the wide open spaces and the lack of trees. We have grand vistas, but this is a naturally occurring prairie and the native plants are forbs, cacti, yucca, and short grasses. There are no trees native to the high plains. Every tree or shrub you find here has been introduced. They may be native to Texas, but not to this particular region.

The plants native to this semi-arid environment tend to have small, light gray or blue-gray leaves that have a waxy surface.

GOOD TREES FOR WEST TEXAS

Texas redbud	*Cercis canadensis* var. *Texensis*
Mexican redbud	*Cercis canadensis* var. *Mexicana*
Flowering crabapples	*Malus* sp.
Purple leaf plum	*Prunus cerasifera atropurpurea* 'Krauter Vesuvius'
Chaste tree	*Vitex agnus-castus*
Golden-rain tree	*Koelreuteria paniculata*
Desert willow	*Chilopsis linearis*
Chitalpa	*Chilopsis linearis* X *Catalpa speciosa*
Cherry laurel	*Prunus caroliniana*
Scotch pine	*Pinus sylvestris*
Austrian pine	*Pinus nigra*
Aleppo pine	*Pinus halepensis*
Texas red oak	*Quercus shumardii texensis*
Bur oak	*Quercus macrocarpa*
Cedar elm	*Ulmus crassifolia*

This is a mechanism that helps the plant reflect light, resist heat, and conserve moisture. Other survival techniques include a deep taproot and late summer dormancy.

Plants with large, tender leaves won't do well here. It is extremely stressful for them because a large leaf surface dries out so quickly. A constant breeze, combined with low ambient humidity, dries out everything.

What kinds of native grasses can you grow here?

Buffalo grass (*Buchloë dactyloides*) is an excellent turf grass. As domestic water prices contin-ue to rise and we have less available water, choosing a drought-resistant grass becomes more and more important. There are a surprising number of bluegrass lawns in this area, but it takes an amazing amount of effort. When people realize what it costs to maintain a Bermuda grass lawn, they're more willing to look at alternatives, such as buffalo grass. You can have a buffalo grass lawn here and maintain it with the natural rainfall if you're willing to let it go dormant at the end of the summer. It's a nice, fine-textured turf grass that is non-invasive. This is even available as a sod now.

Other native grasses that you can use include blue grama grass (*Bouteloua gracilis*) and western wheat grass.

Because it is so flat here—from Lubbock to Amarillo is only an 800-foot change in elevation—we encourage people to do some berming (forming small hills or mounds) in their landscapes and to enhance these with some of the grasses.

What are some good ground covers for the area?

For large areas that are irrigated, some of the best are liriope 'Big Blue', English ivy, germander (*Teucrium chamaedrys*), and vinca (*Vinca major*). Euonymus (*Euonymus coloratus*) is sometimes used, but it is subject to infestations of scale and it is difficult to get it to lay down and cover well. The prostrate juniper does well but it does not compete well enough to discourage weed invasion, making it a high-maintenance plant. The sedums perform best in a shady area where they will not bloom, therefore avoiding the die-out that happens after the plant blooms.

Some of the deciduous ground covers we use are Virginia creeper (*Parthenocissus quinquefolia*), Oxalis (*Oxalis* sp.), and dwarf plumbago (*Ceratostigma plumbaginoides*).

What about perennials?

Many of the sages are good, including *Salvia greggii*, which adapts well here. It's an excellent place to grow many of the gray-green-leafed plants such as artemisias. 'Powis Castle' is one of my favorites. Anything that gets mildew in the East generally does well for us here.

Other good perennials, with irrigation, include daylilies (*Hemerocallis*), red valerian (*Centranthus ruber*), *Veronica* 'Sunny Border Blue', mealycup sage (*Salvia farinacea*), Mexican bush sage (*Salvia leucantha*), goldenrod (*Solidago* sp.), Dusty miller (*Senecio cineraria*), blanket flower (*Gaillardia* x *grandiflora*), Mexican hat (*Ratibida columnifera*), Russian sage (*Perovskia atriplicifolia*), dahlia, coreopsis, and butterfly weed (*Asclepias tuberosa*).

What trees are good to include in the landscape here?

Eastern redbuds, especially the Texas redbud (*Cercis canadensis* var. *Texensis*). It is an under-story tree. There is even a more western form that occurs down into Mexico, *C.c.* var. *Mexicana*.

Flowering crabapples, purple leaf plum (*Prunus cerasifera atropurpurea* 'Krauter Vesuvius'), chaste tree (*Vitex agnus-castus*), golden-rain tree (*Koelreuteria paniculata*), desert willow

(*Chilopsis linearis*), chitalpa
(*Chilopsis linearis* × *Catalpa
speciosa*), cherry laurel (*Prunus
caroliniana*), Scotch pine (*Pinus
sylvestris*), Austrian pine (*Pinus
nigra*), and aleppo pine (*Pinus
halepensis*).

Large shade trees include
Texas red oak (*Quercus
shumardii texensis*), escarpment
live oak (*Quercus reniformis*), and
bur oak (*Quercus macrocarpa*).

The native cedar elm (*Ulmus
crassifolia*) is good, but not the
Siberian elm. The native elm is
an autumn seeder, with high horizontal branching and a good
crotch structure that is important
with our high winds.

**Which shrubs are good to
include?**

We can't grow rhododendrons
and azaleas, which need acidic,
moist soils. We can't even grow
these as container plants. Azaleas
need constant moisture, but not
wet feet. For spring color we recommend shrubs such as forsythia
(*Forsythia* × *intermedia*), and
flowering quince (*Chaenomeles
lagenaria*).

**Do you have any other
advice for people who want to
garden in the Lubbock area?**

Learn as much as you can
about the area. If you don't
know the answer to something,
consult an expert.

ROSA FINSLEY
*Cedar Hill: King's Creek
Landscaping*

Rosa Finsley is a woman who can
move, if not mountains, then at
least very large rocks. Both a
licensed landscape architect and
a knowledgeable plant person,
Rosa designs landscapes for people who want to use native plants
among natural materials such as
rocks and water. Her landscapes
evoke feelings of both tranquility
and interest. Although she has
designed many different kinds of
landscapes, she is probably best
known for her natural landscapes
that include rocks and stones,
some of which weigh as much as
ten tons.

Rosa's extensive knowledge of
plants resulted in the establish-
ment of King's Creek Gardens,
an outstanding specialty nursery
in Cedar Hill, near Dallas. Her
design and installation company,
King's Creek Landscaping, has
won many design awards.

Rosa and her husband have
traveled all over the world,
studying plants, gardens, and
landscapes and how people interact with them. Trips to Japan
and China have resulted in a
broad knowledge of formal as
well as naturalized landscape
concepts, which Rosa has managed to incorporate into the

gardens that she designs in this country.

In addition to her formal training and extensive travel experience, she has also created animal habitats at the Dallas Zoo, a job that she says helped to create a sensitivity to what makes animals—and people—feel right at home.

Well respected in both the horticultural and design communities, Rosa finds her skills in high demand as she travels throughout the western United States designing gardens.

How did your work at the Dallas Zoo creating animal habitats influence your work today as a landscape architect?

It really colored my whole philosophy of design. In making the animal habitats, I studied the animals and tried to determine what it would take to make them feel comfortable enough to thrive and reproduce. I had to constantly ask myself, "What makes this particular animal feel at home? What would help make them live healthily and happily?" I studied not only the animals, but also the natural areas to which they were indigenous and then asked myself questions such as, "How does a jungle feel? Or a rocky outcrop?" I did whatever I could to not only make it look

right, but feel right too.

The idea of creating these habitats of comfort has stayed with me. As I design landscapes, particularly in a city like Dallas, I'm always looking for a way to soften it and to help people get back to their roots. I try to create a landscape in which they can feel comfortable.

Where do you find inspiration for the landscapes you create?

My husband, Charles, worked for the Museum of Natural History in Dallas and studied natural areas all over the state of Texas. I often traveled with him and found what I called "jewel pockets." These were small areas that, usually for a variety of reasons, made me feel good. Sometimes it was the spatial relationship, other times it was the color or texture of the plant material. Each different habitat offered a different inspiration.

For example, in some areas of West Texas you will find huge rocks and a trickle of water which might turn out to be the heart of the entire landscape. In East Texas, the most important element might be the

Tithonia and butterfly

towering pines. In most areas, for me, the feeling of being surrounded or enclosed seemed important. I don't like being on a flat, open plain. I prefer to be surrounded by Nature and to feel immersed in the landscape. For example, it was hard for me to adjust to the landscape around Lubbock, where I went to school, because it was so flat and open. We were always looking for vertical relief. One of our professors joked that they shouldn't even put the electricity wires underground because we needed the poles to give us something to look at in the air.

You never know what you're going to learn, but put yourself in a position to learn whatever is offered.

Can you give an example of a landscape that you've designed based on a natural area you've seen?

There is a beautiful natural pool in the Big Bend area. It has all the perfect elements that they tell you about in landscape design school. No two sides are alike, and it has guard stones where the water comes in. It's like a path created from centuries and centuries of water cutting its way through the rocks. A gravel bed on one side creates a gentle, welcoming approach, and on the opposite side are towering rocks with fabulous plants growing out of the cracks, all of which makes a dramatic backdrop. It was all very different from a traditional water garden, which is usually just a flat pool surrounded by a necklace of rocks.

What we learned from that natural landscape was that everything can't be the same on all sides with no background or foreground. An approach on one side and a view on the other is important, and a careful combination of the kinds and abundance of plant material is also critical. In some places, plant material is naturally more sparse. For example, where it is rocky, plants can only grow in cracks and crevices. In other places, it is more lush.

In general, I suggest that people take the most important elements from the natural spots that speak to them and re-create these in their own landscapes. You can't rebuild the same thing, but you can analyze what you like about different jewel pockets.

You design not only native landscapes, but Japanese Gardens as well. Is your approach similar to both of these?

Yes. When I realized that I really liked naturalistic landscaping, we traveled to Japan and China to see what they were doing there. First we traveled into the wild areas where poets and artists have been inspired for thousands of years, then we went to the gardens to see how they had interpreted these natural areas. We found that Chinese and Japanese gardens are totally different because their wild areas are so different. In Japan, the island is igneous rock, which joins vertically, so they have many rocks that are taller than they are wide. In China, the areas considered most beautiful are based on limestone, sedimentary rocks, which are horizontal. In some areas, these rocks are then magnificently eroded into fantastic shapes.

The gardens in China and Japan both reflect the natural areas found in each country, but the geological makeup of the two countries has resulted in distinctly different kinds of native landscapes. And thus the gardens, which are patterned after these natural areas, are also very different from one another.

We can learn from this by taking a good look at the kinds of natural areas we are trying to depict in our gardens and determining what forces really shaped

and made them what they are. Using this as a basis gives the feeling of integrity to the landscape design. It will feel right even if everyone who sees it does not know why.

Do you have advice for someone who wants to design a naturalistic landscape?

There are two main ways to do this. First, look at what other people in your area have done, and second, study the surrounding natural areas. There is an Italian gentleman, Franco Iritini, who is in charge of our installations, and he gave me some great advice the other day. He said, "Steal with your eyes." That's what we do, both with nature and with other gardens. We're always looking for something that looks pleasing to us.

Understanding a natural area can be a lifelong project. First, you must look at the geology. What kind of rock formations are here? What kind of soil? Then look at the plant material and its response to the soil. Don't just look at what grows, but also at how it grows. Do the trees grow in clumps or do they grow singly as they do on the high plains? For example, live oaks grow in motts, or clumps, because new trees spring up from the roots. Usually the center one is taller because it's older, but then they

all take up interesting shapes
because they are reaching for
light, leaning away from the
mother tree. The entire clump
takes on a rounded shape and
the colony takes on a character.

Look at the grasses to determine what grows and where. In
this area, just south of Dallas,
we're basically a prairie, although
we do have trees growing in
drainage areas too. Where we
have cliffs, we generally have
more trees because groundwater
is draining out through those
cliffs.

To duplicate this feel in a
home landscape, you could treat
the lawn area as a pocket prairie,
using a turf grass such as buffalo
grass. Then you could have a
transition zone with taller grasses
and wildflowers as you approach
a wooded area, which could basically form a border around a
backyard.

In our particular area, we are
fortunate because we are the
dividing line between moist East
Texas and dry West Texas, and
we can grow a blend of species.
It's an exciting place to garden.
When we design a landscape, one
of the first things we consider is
the amount of water available. If
it is a dry, rocky site, we'll use
more western plant material. If it
is good, rich bottomland, we'll
use more plants from East Texas.

**What are some of the plants
that you really like to use in
the landscape?**

For woody plant material, I
like a variety of small ornamental
trees, such as native Mexican
plums, redbuds, rusty blackhaw,
rough-leaved dogwood, and
hollies.

For herbaceous material, I
love showy things such as coreopsis and many of the salvias,
purple coneflower, and native
grasses such as Lindheimer and
Gulf Coast muhly. We use not
only native Texas plants, but
many things that are coming in
from Mexico that we're now
testing in the Dallas area to
determine their hardiness.

The National Wildflower
Research Center has certainly
been a good public relations tool
for the use of native plants. The
new center in Austin is a wonderful display area, showing how
the architecture and the landscape can complement one
another.

**What are some of the stum-
bling blocks to designing a
naturalistic landscape?**

I find that the biggest mistakes people make are in short-
cutting the prep work and not
choosing appropriate plant material for their region. Just because
of human nature, the person
doing the work should not be

the one deciding what should be done. Creating a landscape involves a lot of plain hard work, and if you design your landscape yourself, you might take short-cuts in the preparation. Creating good drainage and soil composition is critical to the success of the landscape.

Another mistake is in getting the plant material before the planting areas have been prepared. We all do it, especially if you love plants. You'll see something that you just have to have, then you'll go home and try to find a spot for it. I've determined that there are two kinds of gardeners. One uses plants to make a design, and the other treats the garden as a place to put their favorite plants. You have the best results when you can combine the two philosophies.

What if you've inherited a garden that wasn't prepared correctly to begin with? Is there anything you can do years after the fact?

Sometimes yes, and sometimes no. It depends on what the flaw is. If it's something really critical, such as poorly drained soil, you might have to go back and dig it up to correct it because it will never get better. But sometimes you can work with what you have and simply change the kind of plant material you use. For

example, if you have poorly drained soils, you can use bog plants that like wet feet, such as wax myrtle and Louisiana iris. If you like the overall design, but need better soil, add 2 to 4 inches of compost each year on top of the soil and mulch where you have room.

Creating a landscape involves a lot of hard work. Don't take shortcuts in the preparation stage. Creating good drainage and soil composition is critical to the success of the landscape.

If you are building a house and have a native landscape to work with, how do you preserve what is already there?

Go slowly. Be careful and figure out what was there originally, and don't destroy any more than you have to. Use what is already there. It's there because it's growing where it wants to. Try to enhance the character of the original landscape and it will make your garden very unique— and easier to maintain. Be especially careful of the tree roots that extend beyond the drip line. Add 2 to 4 inches of compost and coarse mulch over the root

---

STEPS FOR DEVELOPING A NATURAL LANDSCAPE

- Go slowly.
- Determine what is already growing in your area.
- Enhance the character of the original landscape.
- Make your landscape unique and easy to maintain.
- Protect any existing plants, including tree roots, while constructing buildings.

---

zone to feed and protect from compaction during construction. Put plywood over this in areas where the builder will be driving machinery.

Any other advice for creating a habitat for people?

The key is knowledge. You can't know what you're going to learn, but put yourself into a position to learn whatever is offered. Prowl the woods and keep your eyes open. Visit natural areas, parks, wildlife refuges. Go to a place that makes you feel good and try to figure out why. You might be the only one who feels the connection, but that's enough. Don't be afraid to try new things and never quit learning.

ANNE MCGRATH
Austin: Landscape Designer

Anne McGrath's suburban garden in Austin is a wonderful example of how the wise use of plants and resources can result in the creation of a place of beauty and graceful design. Although Anne knew a great deal about color and design from her formal training, the gardening challenges she faced made it necessary to stretch her skills so that she could create the garden of her dreams based on the reality of limited water and unlimited deer.

Foremost among the ideas that she implemented in her garden was the concept of "xeriscaping," the practice of gardening to conserve water and protect the environment. Anne became so well-known for her successful xeriscape gardening that she began working closely with a local committee which promotes this concept.

Anne now spends much of her time designing gardens for other people. Although her formal training is in the fashion industry rather than in landscape design, she says that whether you're designing clothes or a garden, the same principles apply. "Color is color," she says, and to prove her point, she has filled her small

Austin garden with the most beautiful color combinations imaginable. After studying art history and interior design at the University of Texas, Anne realized that her real love lay in the art of the garden. So, she attended all the lectures and classes that she could find, and read as much about gardening in Texas as she possibly could. A real source of

Viola

inspiration for her was Sally and Andy Wasowski's book, *Native Texas Plants.*

To round out her garden design education, she took a course in France with the well-known English landscape designer John Brookes and "read a million books." She says, "To learn design, you can read books from anywhere. For plant selection, you should really stay with local publications."

What did your yard look like when you first moved in?

Before I started the garden, everything was grass. Then I began putting in little theme gardens. One of the first was a white garden, but the deer have eaten just about everything out of that. I don't have nearly as many flowers as I used to because of the deer. It's sometimes frustrating to try to garden here because of them. I usually spend most of my gardening time in the back where it is fenced and the deer can't come in. Gardening in Texas can sometimes be challenging. Not only do I have deer, I also have to put up with armadillos, fire ants, tarantulas, and killer bees.

When did you start your garden here in Austin?

About seven years ago. My goal is to use the live oak trees as a screen for the street, and to try to re-create the rest of the yard to make it look like it might have before the bulldozers came in. Year by year, I've cut down on the amount of lawn I have so that now, the only turf that I have left is on the septic drain field.

I have been very involved with the local xeriscape organization, so I am very aware of water usage. I still use water on some plants, but taking away turf grass is a wonderful way to cut down on water usage in the landscape.

What is xeriscaping and what are some of the basic elements?

Xeriscaping is creating a

landscape that conserves water and protects the environment. A careful selection of plant materials and the appropriate grouping of plants is key to a xeriscape landscape.

Did you have to work with the soils here?

As a rule, yes, but I couldn't do a lot of prep work out front because I was gardening under the oak trees. The roots are shallow, so I couldn't do much digging. Basically, I took the turf off, put down organic matter and compost, and began to plant. I never till when I make a new bed, I just add tons of organic matter. Our soils are generally quite alkaline, but over the years I've added so much mulch and compost that I've succeeded, somewhat, in changing the composition of the soil.

How did you design the front garden?

I tried to use a good combination of understory and low-growing plants under the live oak trees. Most of the trees that I've put in are native, including many that produce berries, such as Carolina buckthorn, Texas redbud, and Barbados cherry. I also have put in some native grasses that do well in the shade, such as inland sea oats and Gulf Coast muhly. Other shrubs include Mexican plum and native moun-

> A FEW PLANTS THAT
> DEER WON'T
> USUALLY EAT
>
> Salvias
> Barberry
> Oregano
> Thyme
> Holly ferns
> Ornamental grasses
> Iris
> Yaupon holly

tain laurel, which produces great purple blooms in spring. I have a lot of salvia in this bed because the deer don't generally eat salvia. Some of my favorites are *S. leucantha*, which takes the shade well, *S. miniata*, *S. mexicana*, and *S. vanhouttii*, which seems to need more sun than some of the others.

Are there any other plants that the deer seem to avoid?

It depends on the year and what else is available and how hungry they are. In general, they don't eat barberry, oregano, thyme, holly ferns, ornamental grasses, iris, or the yaupon hollies.

How is the back garden different?

I started with the pond and wanted to take up as much room as possible with the water garden so I wouldn't have to mow the grass. This area is all fenced so this is where I can grow all the plants that the deer would eat elsewhere. I actually designed this garden as a class project while studying in France, and it's worked out just about like I thought it would, for it's based on an English garden design. It's very full and lush and in the late summer, if we've had a lot of rain, it looks like a jungle garden with all the growth and big vines.

Think about color combina- tions before you buy plants. Although you can use almost any color, it's nice to limit yourself to just a few. Color repetition is important in the garden, so use the same colors or color combinations thorughout your garden to create a pleasing effect.

This is a garden where wildlife—except deer—are wel- comed. We always have frogs in the pond, and birds, butterflies, and dragonflies. A blue heron comes here once a year in early spring. It's fun to see him because he's so big. We also have raccoons in the pond periodically.

What are some of the vines you use?

I use a good bit of clematis, evergreen confederate jasmine, Lady Bank's rose, thunbergia, passion flower, and the pink coral vine, which grows high in the trees—you can see it from the house. I love the cross vine, *Bignonia*, and wisteria. When the two bloom together, you have this wonderful purple and orange combination that is stunning.

I also try to use a good num- ber of annual vines, such as morning glory, hyacinth bean (*Dolichos lablab*), and moon- flower.

Are there basic rules about using color in the garden that would help a home owner design his or her own garden?

Think about color combina- tions before you buy plants. You can use all colors but it's nice to limit yourself. Think about what colors go with your house. Repetition is important, so use the same color combinations over and over again in your garden. Using complementary colors in a grouping creates a very pleasing effect.

Remember that color comes from more than flowers. Stems, foliage (particularly variegated leaves), bark, berries, and fruit all offer color for the garden.

Is there always something in bloom in this garden?

Yes. It looks different in all the

THE SEVEN PRINCIPLES OF A XERISCAPE

Planning and design. Developing a landscape plan is the first and most important step in a successful xeriscape. A properly planned xeriscape takes into account the regional and microclimatic conditions of the site, existing vegetation and topographical conditions, the intended use of the garden and the desires of the property owner, and the zoning or grouping of plant materials by their water needs. A landscape plan also allows landscaping to be done in phases. Many individuals can develop their own plan, but for best results, consult a landscape professional.

Soil analysis. Soils vary from site to site and even within a given site. A soil analysis based on random sampling provides information that enables proper selection of plants and any soil amendments needed. When appropriate, soil amendments can enhance the health and growing capabilities of the landscape by improving water drainage, moisture penetration, and a soil's water-holding capability.

Appropriate plant selection. Plant selection should be based on the plant's adaptability to the landscaped area, the effect desired, and the ultimate size, color, and texture of the plants. Plants should be arranged to achieve the aesthetic effect desired and grouped in accordance with their respective water needs. Most plants have a place in a xeriscape. Maximum water conservation can be achieved by selecting the plants that require a minimal amount of supplemental watering in a given area. Landscape professionals can be of assistance when selecting plant material.

Practical turf areas. The type and location of turf areas should be selected in the same manner as all other plantings. Turf shouldn't be treated as fill-in material, but rather as a major planned element of the xeriscape. Because many turf varieties require supplemental watering more or less often than other types of landscape plants, turf should be placed where it can be irrigated separately. Although turf areas provide many practical benefits in a landscape, how and where it is used can result in a significant reduction in water use.

Efficient irrigation. Watering only when plants need water and watering deeply encourages deeper root growth, resulting in a healthier and more drought-tolerant landscape. If a landscape requires regular watering, or if an irrigation system is desired, the system should be well planned and managed. Water can be conserved through the use of a properly designed irrigation system. Consult landscape and irrigation professionals when planning irrigation for a xeriscape.

Use of mulches. Mulches applied and maintained at appropriate depths in planting beds help soils retain moisture, reduce weed growth, and prevent erosion. Mulch can be used where conditions aren't adequate for growing quality turf or ground covers. Mulches are typically wood bark chips, wood grindings, pine straw, nutshells, small gravel, or shredded landscape clippings.

Appropriate maintenance. Proper landscape and irrigation maintenance preserve and enhance a quality xeriscape. When the first six principles have been followed, maintenance of a xeriscape is easier and less expensive than for a traditional landscape. A xeriscape is healthier and uses a minimal amount of water, so fewer fertilizers, pesticides, and other chemicals are needed to maintain it.

seasons, although I think I probably like spring the best. In spring, I have a lot of pink and lavender in the garden from roses, sweet peas, larkspur, snapdragons, bluebonnets, violas, and pansies. I also have a lot of penstemons that are beautiful in spring and little irises that are low growing.

Do you spray for pests and disease?

This is a totally organic garden. If I do have problems, for example, with a rose having mildew, I just ignore it, or if the garden is going to be on tour, I pick the affected leaves. I water things by hand, and use this time to wash off a lot of bugs. That way I can water only when the plants need it. Besides, it's my relaxation.

How would you advise someone who is trying to begin a garden?

First, I would tell them to consult with someone who knows gardening in their area. Then I would encourage them to go to all the local lectures or classes that he or she could. Ask questions. Become informed. Enjoy your garden.

Resources

Publications

BOOKS

The American Horticultural Society Encyclopedia of Garden Plants. New York: Macmillan Publishers, 1989.

Brookes, John. *The Book of Garden Design*. New York: Macmillan, 1991.

———. *The Garden Book*. New York: Crown Publishers, Inc., 1984.

———. *The Small Garden*. New York: Crown Publishers, Inc., 1991.

Church, Thomas D. *Gardens Are for People*, 2nd edition. New York: McGraw Hill, 1983.

Cox, Jeff. *Plant Marriages*. New York: HarperCollins, 1993.

Hobhouse, Penelope. *Color in Your Garden*. Boston: Little Brown, 1985.

Johnson, Hugh. *The Principles of Gardening*. New York: Simon and Schuster, 1984.

Roth, Sally. *Natural Landscaping: Gardening with Nature to Create a Backyard Paradise*. Emmaus, PA: Rodale Press, 1997.

Verey, Rosemary. *Rosemary Verey's Good Planting Plans*. Boston: Little Brown, 1993.

Wasowski, Sally and Andy Wasowski. *Native Texas Plants: Landscaping Region by Region*. Houston: Gulf Publishing, 1997.

Wasowski, Sally and Andy Wasowski. *Native Texas Gardens, Maximum Beauty, Minimum Upkeep*. Houston: Gulf Publishing, 1997.

MAGAZINES

Garden Design
American Society of Landscape Architects
1733 Connecticut Avenue
Washington, D.C. 20009

FLOWERS

GREG GRANT
*Nacogdoches: Stephen F. Austin
University*

Perhaps it was his birthplace that influenced the future career of Greg Grant. Born in the rose capital of the world, Tyler, Texas, Greg decided in the second grade that he wanted to be a plant person for life. "I was Keeper of the Terrarium in first grade," he says, "so I already had some pretty good experience!" Greg classifies his early gardening experiences as magical. "The first time I planted potatoes with my grandfather and put those little tiny pieces of potatoes in the ground and then dug up a whole bunch of potatoes months later, I thought it was pure magic."

Greg went on to earn bachelor's and master's degrees in floriculture and a master's degree in horticulture from Texas A&M University, then spent the next ten years gathering experience and hands-on education all over the world. But his heart remained in East Texas, and when a position at Stephen F. Austin University became available, he came back home to teach in the horticulture department.

"East Texas is a great place to grow plants," he says. He has proven his words by contributing countless new plants to the Stephen F. Austin University Arboretum. Greg's plant passions deal primarily with herbaceous plants—both heirloom and new cultivars.

Narcissus

What recommendations do you have for someone just starting to garden in East Texas?

The first thing you do is face the facts. This is not the north-eastern United States. You cannot grow lilacs, astilbe, hosta, and peonies here because our growing climate is entirely different. We talk about the lilac/crape myrtle line. Above it you grow lilacs, below you grow the crape myrtles. We're definitely below the line and we try to encourage people to plant accordingly. It's not fair to the plant or the gardener to put in a plant that simply won't do well in our region.

But the good news is that there are many, many plants that grow wonderfully well in this region. Many of these are old-fashioned plants that lost favor through the years for one reason or another but that are now making a comeback. For a long time, we thought that plants such as nandinas, orange day-lilies, and cannas were below our level of sophistication.

What are the growing conditions here in Nacogdoches and the surrounding area?

We have both heat and

OUTSTANDING PERENNIALS FOR EAST TEXAS	
Yarrow	*Achillea* spp.
Columbines	*Aquilegia* spp.
Coreopsis (best cultivars)	*C. grandiflora* 'Early Sunrise', 'Baby Sun', 'Sunray'
Daylily	*Hemerocallis* spp.
Double orange daylily	*H. fulva* 'Kwanso'
Iris (bearded, Louisiana, Siberian)	*Iris* spp.
Turk's cap	*Malvaviscus arboreus* var. *drummondii*
Japanese Maiden Grass	*Miscanthus sinensis*
Daffodils	*Narcissus* spp.
Summer phlox	*Phlox paniculata*
Thrift	*Phlox subulata*
Mealycup sage	*Salvia farinacea*
Mexican bush sage	*Salvia leucantha*
Purple Jew / Purple heart	*Tradescantia pallida* 'Purpurea'

humidity, and the combination is often tough on plants. But we have three good growing seasons—spring, summer, and fall. People need to realize that it's better to use different plant material during our hot summers than we use in spring and fall. Many of the more traditional summer annuals will not survive here, but there are many plants that thrive in our summer heat, mostly tropicals such as coleus, lantana, and fire bush (*Hamelia patens*). Some perennial tropical plants, such as Mexican heather (*Cuphea hyssopifolia*), are used as annuals here.

We have tropical conditions here during summer. The rainfall is high—between 45 and 60 inches annually—and we have high heat. We are in horticultural Zone 8, however, meaning it does get cold enough in winter to kill back the tropical plants.

Our soils are fairly acidic, usually with a pH between 5.2 and 6.2.

Are growing conditions here similar to those in other areas of the Southeast?

We're almost identical to Alabama, Mississippi, and Georgia south of Atlanta, with two major differences. First, it gets hotter here. We can get temperatures consistently around the 100-degree mark in the summer

with very warm nights. That's why we can't grow shrubs such as rhododendrons, kalmias, or daphnes.

Second, it heats up fast and cools down fast due to the southern influences from Mexico and the Gulf in the summer, and the "blue northers" in the winter. In winter, the winds out of Canada come straight down, causing the temperatures to fluctuate dramatically. In February, it can be around 85° and then we'll get an Arctic blast from Canada and it will drop to 25°. Without any kind of hardening-off period, that's extremely hard on the plants.

Those temperature fluctuations really affect the kinds of plants we can grow here. We regularly suffer freeze damage on deciduous magnolias, tea roses, crape myrtles, etc. We deal with it by trying to limit fall and winter growth. As a rule, it's best not to prune or fertilize tender plants in the fall.

On the other hand, many of the Mediterranean plants that would thrive in our heat can't take the humidity, so many of the gray-leafed plants such as lamb's ear, artemisia, and columbines just don't grow well here without extensive soil modification.

How do you need to amend the soils here?

The soils are low in nitrogen and low in nutrients in general, but they drain well. Because it rains a lot, the nutrients leach out of the soil and fertility is a major factor. The soils are not terrible, as a general rule. We either have sandy loam or clay, but we always recommend adding organic matter such as compost, peat moss, or pine bark. We suggest that you feed the plants with something— either organic or chemical, but add something. We preplant with fertilizer and side dress with manures and use lawn fertilizer for trees, shrubs, and flowers.

For ornamentals, we generally don't worry about the acidity because so many of the flowering plants are either tolerant of, or prefer acidic soils. We usually lime the vegetable gardens, however.

What types of flowering shrubs can you grow?

We use a lot of southern indica azaleas, spirea, Indian hawthorn, and many hollies such as Chinese and yaupon.

Are there some good bulbs to use in this area?

Yes, particularly some of the old-fashioned ones that have stood the test of time. Many of the narcissus species are native to southern France, Spain, and surrounding Mediterranean areas and love our dry summers and wet winters. The most common narcissi were brought over from Europe by the early colonists, and many of these are now naturalized in old homesites and cemeteries. Others that thrive here include snowflakes, spider lilies, and oxblood lilies.

What's the difference between narcissus, daffodils, and jonquils?

They are all different species of the genus *Narcissus*. True jonquils have dark green, round, rushlike leaves and clusters of small, fragrant, early, yellow blossoms. The plant commonly called "narcissus" refers to the early-blooming white variety, *Narcissus tazetta*, and includes the paper-whites. Daffodils are usually yellow, single trumpet flowers of *Narcissus pseudonarcissus*. Large-flowered forms of the latter are the least suited for naturalizing here.

Which of these are best for naturalizing?

The early blooming, cluster flowered species and hybrids. They tend to be small flowered, and because they bloom so early (January through March) the foliage matures before mowing begins. To naturalize successfully, the foliage must be allowed to grow, mature, and age naturally without being cut back.

When is the best time to plant *Narcissus*?

You can plant new bulbs when they are dormant and available (June through October) or transplant old ones in mid- to late summer after they have gone dormant. Be sure to mark the bulbs that you want to transplant because once the foliage yellows and dies it will be difficult to

BEST NATURALIZING
BULBS FOR TEXAS

Narcissus jonquilla—yellow, fragrant blooms in February
Narcissus X *odorus* (Greg considers the best)—yellow, fragrant blooms in February
Narcissus X *intermedius*—creamy yellow, fragrant blooms in February
Narcissus tazetta 'Grand Primo'—creamy white, fragrant blooms in February
Narcissus tazetta var. *papyraceus* (paper-whites)—pure white, fragrant blooms in December and January. Performs best in southern and coastal regions of the state (below I-10).
Narcissus tazetta var. *orientalis*—white and yellow bicolor, fragrant blooms in January–February. Best along the coast only.

remember where the bulbs are. All bulbs in the South should be planted before October, if possible, to take advantage of fall root growth. Because our bulbs bloom earlier, we have to plant them earlier, otherwise they will be stunted.

You coauthored *The Southern Heirloom Garden* with William Welch. What is it about old-fashioned plants that caught your attention?

Although it's only human nature for a gardener to want to try new and unusual plants in their gardens, I think that the foundation of the garden should be the tried and true, historically adapted plant material. I think that wide-swinging trends and favoritism should not be allowed into mainstream gardening. They only confuse the common gardener.

The heirloom plants, those that have lived and grown for centuries, some without any care at all, will work for us today as well. I admit, I talk to my plants. I tell them that they either pull their weight, or I'll pull them up and throw them away. After years of searching for the ideal plants, I finally found them right where they have been since I began the search.

Heirloom plants are not good because they are old, they are old

GOOD OLD-FASHIONED PLANTS FOR TEXAS

Chinese trumpet creeper	*Campsis grandiflora*
Cockscomb	*Celosia argentea cristata*
Crinums	*Crinum bulbispermum* and hybrids
Milk and wine lilies	*Crinum* × *herbertii*
Byzantine gladiolus	*Gladiolus byzantinus*
St. Joseph's lily	*Hippeastrum vittatum*
Blue Roman hyacinths	*Hyacinthus orientalis* var. *albulus*
Lantana	*Lantana* sp.
Turk's cap	*Malaviscus arboreus* var. *drummondii*
Four o'clocks	*Mirabilis jalapa*
Campernelle jonquil	*Narcissus* × *odorus*
Grand Primo narcissus	*Narcissus tazetta* 'Grand Primo'
Flowering tobacco	*Nicotiana alata*
Old-fashioned petunias	*Petunia* × *hybrida*
Magenta-pink phlox	*Phlox paniculata*
Purple Jew	*Tradescantia pallida* 'Purpurea'

because they are good. It's really comforting to know that I don't have to worry about weeds, pests, drought, and freezes. These guys have seen them all come and go, yet still persisted. All I have to do is create a pleasing design with them.

What is the difference between the terms old-fashioned, heirloom, and antique?

They are essentially interchangeable in the horticultural world, although according to the American Rose Society, a rose is considered an old garden rose if it was introduced before 1867. Nonsense, as far as I'm concerned. Many of our best roses (Teas, Chinas, and Polyanthas) are not old enough to be antique or new enough to be modern. But, does this actually matter in the garden? In my opinion, heirloom usually means that it has been passed down through generations, and both Forrest Gump and Tom Bodett agree that "old" is if your mamma grew it and "antique" is if your grandma grew it.

EDDIE HENDERSON
*Amarillo: Amarillo Botanical
Gardens*

Born and raised in Amarillo,
Eddie Henderson is now raising
his two sons in this same town
and with the same love of gardening with which he was raised.
"My maternal grandmother
always gardened," Eddie remembers. "She loved to hoe. Some
families have to hide the brandy
when grandma comes to visit,
but we had to hide the hoe! If it
was green and not blooming, my
grandmother considered it a
weed and would chop it down.
My paternal grandparents were
avid gardeners. They were from
Oklahoma and they plowed up
both the front and the back yards
to put in wonderful vegetable
gardens. Gardening was always
such an important part of my life
that I'm trying
to pass on this
same passion to
my sons. They
don't necessarily
appreciate working
in the yard and the
garden now, but as I
see it, it takes a while to
learn to love to garden."

Today, Eddie and his
wife are in an unusual gardening situation for
Amarillo—big trees and a lot

Iris

of shade, unlike most Amarillo
gardens, which receive full sun.
But shady conditions are not
conducive to vegetable gardening. Instead, they have planted
flowers and shade-loving plants
to create their own garden
haven.

Eddie's love of plants and
gardening led him to join the
board of the Amarillo Botanical
Gardens and to serve as its president, a post that he has held
since 1996. One of his duties as
president is to write a monthly
column for the Botanical
Gardens newsletter. In April
1996 he wrote, "I'm drawn more
strongly to the garden as my sons
become young men and demand
less coddling. I've concluded that
caring for a garden satisfies the
unstoppable habits of child rear-
ing—the caring and tending, the
watching and anticipating. After
all, by the time you've gotten
them reared, you've become
rather good at it. Wouldn't it
be a shame to let all of that
trial and error go to waste?
I'm sure that old men raise
vegetables and old women
have cats because their children
have grown up."

**What is it like to garden in
Amarillo, Texas?**
We have a very unique
climate in that it is extreme. We

have cold, windy winters and hot, dry summers. It's a challenge for both plants and people. We have to constantly adjust our thinking so that we choose plant material wisely. For example, if a plant catalog says a plant needs a lot of water and protection from the wind, we know immediately that it is not a plant for Amarillo.

People need to educate themselves about gardening in the Texas Panhandle. Too often they will go to the landscaping department at a discount store and see beautiful plants, which they buy by the basketful. Many of them are simply not suited for our area. The specialty stores seem to have a greater knowledge about suitable plant material.

I guess there are some advantages to living in this climate—if the cold doesn't kill the bugs in winter, the dry will get them in summer.

Can you describe winters here?

They are often severe. Many times the days are warm and the nights are clear and cold. But when we have bad weather, it can be extremely bad. We can't

rely on horticultural zones as indicators for what we should plant because zones are based on averages and on the average, our weather is mild—but it's the extremes that kill plants. The other problem is that the cold weather comes on so quickly. It can be in the fifties during the day and drop to zero at night.

How about the summers?

The same is true of the summers: It's the extremes that make gardening in the Texas Panhandle so difficult. It's usually mild, but the temperatures can reach 105° with high, drying winds. It's the extremes that make the climate interesting—and I like that.

What is your frost-free growing season?

The old-timers always say to wait until Mother's Day. For years I would go out and put in bedding plants on a nice, warm spring day until I finally accepted the fact that if you plant early, you are probably going to have to plant again. Spring, meaning May and June, are our best gardening months and that's when our gardens are at their peak. We generally get good rains from mid- to late May.

In fall, we usually get our first hard freeze at Halloween.

Are there plants that are well adapted to this climate?

You have to plant things that thrive in a dry climate and that don't require a great deal of water. In most places you can just use supplemental irrigation to grow what you want, but not here because the air is so dry. By August the air is so hot and dry that it doesn't matter how much water you get to the roots, the leaves will still not get enough moisture.

We believe in the school of trial and error. We suggest that when people want to try a new plant for their yard or garden, that they buy a dozen of the same plant because it is so difficult to guess what is going to grow well. Every yard has little microclimates, one of which might be just right for growing a particular plant. You can't just go by the books or what someone else does. If you want to grow a plant, you'll have to try it yourself in different areas of your own garden.

Do you have favorite plants with which you've had good luck?

I've worked hard with the bearded iris. I thought that they would do well here because it is so dry in the summer and they won't rot. This year I had the most gorgeous plants that were loaded with buds. In the middle of May we had a snow and that was the end of that. I had a garden of green mush. It's those odd, unpredictable bits of weather that are a challenge. The Siberian iris does not do as well as the bearded iris because of the dry climate.

Every yard has little microclimates that might be just right for growing a particular plant. You can't go by the books or what someone else does. If you want to grow a plant, you'll have to try it yourself in different areas of your own garden.

I love Japanese anemones, too. Everyone told me they wouldn't grow here, so I decided to find out. I bought twelve plants and put them in the ground to see if they would make it through the year. I put them in last fall and now I have the most beautiful anemones you'll ever see. I don't really know why. I put them in a fairly protected area in a small enclosed garden and that helps moderate the harsh winter temperatures. I believe that they work well in my particular garden because I found the right niche for them. They're a wonderful plant because they are elegant and different.

In general, the plants that do well in areas such as Santa Fe should do well here. For example, black-eyed Susans and the purple coneflower both do well. There are also many flowering bulbs that do well, such as the alliums—not the giant allium, which I think is sort of a creepy plant, but some of the smaller ones. The hybrid tulips will give you bloom for several years, as will narcissus. We have to plant spring bulbs a little deeper than the growers recommend because of the extreme winter temperatures.

Daylilies do great here and have been adopted as the city's flower. There's even a new cultivar named 'Amarillo'. Roses do well, particularly the old-fashioned varieties. I've never had any real disasters with roses, but I've never had any great successes either. The peonies seem to like the cold weather and bloom a little later than the bearded iris, generally in early June.

The gray- and silver-leafed plants, such as artemisia and lamb's-ear, do well because of the lack of humidity. And we can grow all the common annuals such as salvias, marigold, hollyhocks, and petunias.

Are there flowering shrubs that do well?

Yes, this is a good place for many plants such as lilacs, crab-apples, and redbud. The colder the winter, the better they seem to bloom. They grow better here than they do in Dallas and Houston. Shrubs and trees such as forsythia, crape myrtle, butterfly bush, and weigela perform well, if they are protected. We cannot grow azaleas and rhododendrons, however.

How about evergreen shrubs?

'Nellie R. Stevens' holly is a great one. It doesn't matter how bad the winter is, it comes back like gangbusters. You might lose boxwoods and other kinds of hollies, but not 'Nellie'. The yaupon hollies do pretty well, too, and will get to good size.

Are there ways to protect tender plants to extend the variety of plants you can grow?

Yes. If you want to go to the trouble, you can mulch heavily in winter and wrap shrubs. The city of Amarillo has a large area where they chip and shred limbs and leaves and give it away free as mulch. There are also a lot of feed yards in the area, which means that well-rotted manure is readily available.

TREES AND SHRUBS FOR
AMARILLO

Lilacs
Crabapples
Redbud
Forsythia
Crape myrtle
Butterfly bush
Weigela

One trick that I've had good success with when growing clematis is to take broken pieces of clay pots and spread them around the root area and put mulch on top of that. The clay seems to hold moisture and warmth. Every time I break a clay pot, I put the pieces around the clematis.

Do you have to work with your soils?

I'm convinced that the way to have a good garden is to begin with amending the soil. You should really spend more time on treating the soil than working with plant material. It makes an amazing difference, no matter where you live, if you work to get good soils. The more mulch and manure I add, the better my garden produces.

I do everything organically now. A few years ago, I put snail bait out all over the garden and our dog got into it and almost died. Since then, I've decided that it's just not worth it. I quit using pesticides altogether and I can't see that much difference in the bugs in my garden. It has to be better for you and the environment not to spray all that stuff into the air. I just stay away from plants that seem to have a lot of problems, such as nasturtiums. We don't seem to have a lot of problems with insect pests. I guess there are some advantages to living in this climate—if the cold doesn't kill the bugs in the winter, the dry will get them in the summer.

Are there resources here for people to learn about gardening?

We hope that the Amarillo Botanical Garden will be a major resource. We have a master plan and our vision is to create a three-acre botanical garden. We also hope to have people on staff who can answer questions and work with the public one-on-one with any gardening problems they have. Our primary goal is education; our secondary goal is to create outstanding displays.

Another good resource is the Texas A&M University Extension Service, which has an office here and has developed a good master gardener program.

Do you have any other advice?

Walk around and look at different gardens and decide what looks good to you. Ask questions and read as much as you can. If you want to grow something, buy several plants and put them in different places in your garden to see where they will do best.

Pay attention to design as well and strive for a natural, graceful look. If you follow basic design principles, such as planting in odd numbers, in drifts of three or five, for example, it will look better.

MIKE SHOUP
Brenham: The Antique Rose Emporium

Like many specialty gardeners, Mike Shoup began his horticultural career working with a general retail garden center. "It was in the late seventies, which was a real boom time in Houston. Anything green was selling and I was selling a lot of plants such as photinia and ligustrum," Mike remembers. "When the oil crash of the early eighties hit, plants became a luxury item, and we suffered along with everyone else."

In response to those hard times, Mike decided to introduce native plants into the horticultural industry and experienced some success with oaks, sages, and yaupon hollies. But it was when he began finding old roses in the same tough Texas environment in which he found native plants that he realized their potential worth. It was through selling the old-fashioned, hardy roses of Texas that Mike enjoyed his first real success and found a passion interesting enough to last him a lifetime.

Today, the Antique Rose Emporium is known throughout the United States, and the demonstration gardens that he has established in Brenham and San Antonio, Texas, and Dahlonega, Georgia, are beautiful enough to be ranked among the better botanical gardens of the country.

Rose

Why are antique roses such good plants for Texas gardens?

Texas is a difficult place in which to garden. Climatic concerns can be formidable. We have tremendous droughts and heat in summer, and then in winter, we have "blue northers" come in. It can be 70° during the day for two or three weeks in January and then all of a sudden it can go down to 5° overnight. It's extremely hard on the plants, and anything that survives ought to be a natural selection for a home garden.

When we were out looking for native plants, we noticed that there were many roses that were surviving—and thriving—without any care at all. It was obvious that some of these plants had been there fifty or one hundred years. That's the kind of plant that I wanted to sell—something beautiful to look at and hardy enough to survive our climate.

Where did you find the old-fashioned roses?

Old cemeteries proved to be fruitful hunting grounds for roses, as did old fence lines and homesites. We'd also go visit self-taught gardeners, typically the longtime residents, who often lived in less affluent neighborhoods in town. We began to recognize the kind of garden that would be promising—on the front porch would be thousands of pots with different kinds of plants. It would be the home of someone who loved to grow things. When we talked to them,

which turned out to be one of the best things about this job, they would tell us stories about their roses. Most of them would not know the names, but it would be their grandmother's rose that she brought over from Europe that had been in the family for a long time. Often, they would have passed cuttings around the neighborhood, so you would find the same rose over and over in the same locale.

How did you figure out which roses you had?

In many cases, we didn't. We'd just give them names, often after the people who gave them to us, such as 'Mary Minor' or 'Martha Gonzales'. Or sometimes we'd name them after the place where they were found, such as '29 Pink Buttons', which was one we found off Highway 29, or 'Old Gay Hill', which was found in Gay Hill, Texas.

We also used some of the old catalogs that were popular back at the turn of the century and found some of these same plants listed in these.

How are old-fashioned roses different from modern roses?

When we began dealing with antique roses, we realized that we were dealing with a completely different rose from what was being sold in today's rose market. The rose had managed to change temperament and application in the modern garden. Modern roses are bred for color and long stems; high-centered flowers and stiff forms. This is the kind of flower that will win best of show at an exhibition. Rose breeders had concentrated on attaining these characteristics for so long that they bred out many of the characteristics that we were finding in the older varieties, things such as disease resistance, fragrance, hardiness, and garden form.

What we've been offering for fifteen years now are roses that give home owners a rest from the nurturing and spraying that modern roses require. We are trying to educate people to take a new look at the old roses. Unfortunately, if we ask ten people on the street what they think of roses, nine out of ten will say, "I love roses, but I can't grow them." That is a tragedy. We would like to change this with the return of old garden roses.

Are the old roses really easy to grow?

If we look at some of the old varieties, we find that they grow and survive without any care. That's proved over and over by finding these roses at abandoned homesites. The only thing we

have to do is to educate people as to what the garden rose looks like. No, it doesn't look like the modern rose, which has the "perfect" flower, but they are beautiful in their own right. And they give you lots of color and fragrance and don't require a lot of effort from the gardener once they're in the ground.

How do you use old roses, or garden roses, in the garden?

Our gardens are built around the philosophy that the rose is just another component in the overall garden theme. So much emphasis is placed on modern roses to perform, they are always planted like soldiers in perfectly straight rows. I think it's very boring. Part of the charm of old roses is the nostalgic versatility you get by mixing these roses with other plants, to blend and combine to embellish the architecture of the home, or to mix with perennials, herbs, or annuals to make a garden. In this way, the rose is allowed the same ebb and flow of the other plants. It's just one of the components. It is still the backbone of all our gardens because it is so beautiful and provides so many different traits. We use it as a hedge, a ground cover, or a shrub. We let it climb or cascade.

Around our little 1800s house

here in Brenham, Texas, we've combined herbs and roses to make a cottage garden. We've also used them in a Victorian garden and in many other kinds of gardens. The climbing roses, in particular, give a romantic aspect to a garden, with roses dripping down from pillars or trellises. To walk under them and smell them is a great experience. People come here and get a refreshing look at the rose and the importance they have in the garden.

Y̶ou need to make sure that roses get at least a half day of sun, otherwise the gardener will be disappointed. After that, it doesn't matter what soil type you have, because you can overcome anything by adding soil improvements. We recommend that gardeners put 3 to 4 inches of decomposed organic matter on top of the soil and mix it in with the top 6 to 8 inches.

How do you collect old roses?

I've trained my employees to be rose rustlers, not to pillage or dig them up, but to do search and rescue. We try to protect the shrubs at their original location

and just take cuttings. I encourage everyone to be a rose rustler, because they will find plants that are suited to their own location.

Within the state of Texas, what are the conditions you need for growing the garden roses?

We try to help people get off on the right foot when growing roses, and this means making sure that the plants have at least a half day of sun. Otherwise, the gardener is going to be disappointed. You have to have enough sun. After that, it doesn't matter what soil type you have. It can be sand or clay, alkaline or acidic—these can be overcome by adding soil improvements such as decomposed organic matter, manures, leaf mold, compost, pine bark. We recommend that gardeners apply 3 to 4 inches of this material and mix it in with the top 6 to 8 inches of the soil. That will provide a happy environment for the roses.

You have to keep adding organic matter year after year. You do this as you mulch. Synthetic fertilizers have proven to be very difficult to use in growing roses. If you put in a fertilizer that is high in phosphorous, the plants will take this up in preference to some of the micronutrients that they really need.

This results in a phosphorous toxicity. The best way to overcome this is to create a living environment in the soil so that the microorganisms provide the micronutrients by breaking down the soil. This is the natural way. This releases the nutrients to be taken up by the plants. Over the long term, roses are much happier with just the addition of organic matter. The soil is alive and everything is in much better balance.

Are there areas of Texas that are simply too hot to grow roses?

The heat is usually not a limiting aspect of growing roses. Some of the European varieties get sad and tired in the heat, but many varieties flourish through the summer. They won't put on as many blooms, and will take a rest when it's really hot, but they will still contribute to the garden.

How often should you water?

In a garden situation, we advise watering deeply once a week. In summer, the garden might need more than that, but once a rose is established, 2 inches of water a week ought to be sufficient. Even in times of drought, the rose might lose some of its leaves, but it will come back.

One of the magical things about antique roses is that a gardener can spend as much—or as little—time with them as they want. They can put a big shrub rose in a back area where it doesn't need to look manicured and just let it grow. Or, if they want to keep it trimmed and neat, they can do that as well. You get what you put into it.

How much maintenance do roses need?

It all depends on the gardener. That's what's so magical about these plants. If you put a big shrub rose in a back area where it doesn't need to look manicured, you can just let it grow as if it were growing in a cemetery. If you want to keep it trimmed and neat looking, for instance near the entrance to your home, you can do that as well. We preach a commonsense approach here. You get what you put into it.

For example, we have black spot on a few of our display roses here, because we choose not to spray—we just consider it "early fall color." Black spot is not detrimental to the plant. We just

MIKE SHOUP'S FAVORITE ROSES

China Roses
Chunky shrubs as wide as they are tall. With their thick, heavy foliage and colorful blooms, they make a good focal point for a perennial border or massed together as a hedge.

- 'Cramoisi Supérieur'—Crimson flowers with silvery reverse; rounded shape; almost everblooming in a warm climate. Grows to 3–6 feet.
- 'Archduke Charles'—Full flowers, crimson on outer petals, pink in center. Grows to 3–5 feet.
- 'Ducher'—The only white China rose, with ivory-white blossoms. Good in a container. Grows to 3–5 feet.

Tea Roses
Thought to be a cross between *Rosa chinensis* and *R. gigantea*, teas are named for their scent, which is similar to that of fresh tea leaves. Bushy growth habit, bronzy new growth, profuse blooms, disease resistant.

- 'Adam'—Double salmon pink blooms. Grows to 5–7 feet.
- 'Sombreuil'—Creamy white blossoms are large and flat; considered the hardiest and most vigorous white tea. Grows to 8–12 feet.

- 'Mrs. B. R. Cant'—Large 8-foot shrub with large silvery pink blossoms; blooming nine months of the year.

Noisette Roses
Very "Southern" roses, the result of a cross of 'Old Blush' with a wild musk rose. The following three varieties of these fragrant climbing roses are repeat bloomers, putting on a show on and off throughout the season. Very rewarding for the amount of color they offer.

- 'Rêve D'Or'—Large, loose, double, buff yellow flowers; wonderful fragrance; blooms all season.
- 'Lamarque'—Medium-sized double flowers; white petals with a touch of yellow; vigorous climber.
- 'Mme. Alfred Carrière'—Cupped, double, pink-to-creamy-white flowers. Climbs vigorously to about 20 feet on thornless canes.

Polyantha Roses
Introduced in the late 1800s, these fragrant, versatile garden roses are tighter and more compact than most, growing to 2–3 feet.

- 'Cécile Brünner'—The

"sweetheart rose"; blooms from mid-spring until frost; bushy, compact form with tiny perfect pink blossoms.
- 'Marie Pavié'—Versatile rose for containers or as a low hedge. Pink buds open to creamy white. Grows to 3–4 feet.
- 'La Marne'—Makes a good hedge plant. Pinkish-white flowers are held in loose clusters.

Hybrid Musk Roses
This important group of roses form big, billowing shrubs that cascade over themselves if left unattended. They get bigger and better each year.
- 'Ballerina'—Good for hedges. Has small, single pink flowers with white eyes; grows to be a 5–6 foot shrub.
- 'Penelope'—Massive clusters of pink semi-double flowers. Grows into a 5×5-foot shrub.
- 'Cornelia'—A good climber or specimen plant with long, arching canes. Coral buds open to pink.

don't get hung up about spraying roses. If they lose leaves, it won't mean anything in the overall life cycle of a rose.

How about pruning?

The garden roses are very different from the hybrid teas, which have lots of rules and generally completely ruin the enthusiasm of gardening for many people.

In a garden setting, you simply want to maintain the general form of the plant. You also might want to prune back the shrubs to encourage new and denser growth. So, we tell people to get the hedge trimmers out and cut back once or twice a year before the onset of new growth. We enjoy our fall bloom, so we cut back at the end of the summer. By late October, we get great new growth. It is probably one of the most beautiful times of the year in our garden—and the roses are a major contributor.

Some roses we just shape up, some we might cut down by half. Climbers are different because they have a different growth pattern. They need to adorn something. Put them on a pillar, fence, trellis, or the side of a house and train them to those structures. Some people think that a climbing rose is just going to do what it wants to do, but training is important. There's some effort involved in training these roses, but the results are breathtaking.

LIZ DRUITT
Cedar Hill: Writer and Garden Designer

When asked if she came from a family of Southern gardeners, Liz Druitt laughs, "No! But I do come from a long line of southerners, even if they did come from the south of England and the south of Scotland! The south is definitely an important part of my heritage."

Liz's interest in plants began when she took on a weekend job at the then newly opened Antique Rose Emporium. "I was a real beginner," Liz remembers. "The first day someone handed me a potted plant and told me to go plant it in the garden. I can remember thinking, 'I wonder if I take it out of the pot first or just plant the whole thing?'"

Since that inauspicious beginning, Liz has acquired a remarkable education about plants and gardening. "I've been lucky," she says. "I've been able to work at both the Antique Rose Emporium and with Libbie Winston at the Peaceable Kingdom (the Organic Plant Institute), which I consider two of the finest public gardens in Texas."

But it is a real love and appreciation of plants that keeps Liz in the forefront of the gardening world. As frequent host of the video series *The New Garden,* author of *The Organic Rose Garden,* and coauthor (with Michael Shoup) of *Landscaping with Antique Roses,* she has influenced gardeners throughout the country.

'Snow Carpet' Rose

What is it about roses that really caught your attention?

Roses have to be the most versatile plant in the garden. The blossoms are almost every color, flower form, and fragrance imaginable, and the plants themselves come in an amazing range of sizes, foliage patterns, and growth habits. I only have about 150 different varieties in pots at my house, but even the foliage shows remarkable diversity. It varies from the willowy-looking leaves of the swamp rose, *Rosa palustris,* to the tiny leaves of microminiatures; from the huge, glossy green leaves of hybrid teas to the purple and burgundy foliage of *Rosa glauca.*

With such a huge selection of roses from which to choose, how does a gardener decide which roses to include in his garden?

First, see what's growing in your area already. You can find roses growing anywhere in this country. There is no soil or climate in the United States that is not appropriate for some kind of rose. But that doesn't mean that all roses will do well for you in your particular niche. So, find established rose bushes in your area and ask about them. Go to a local botanical garden and take notes. Write down names of things that appeal to you and ask questions of the staff or volunteers who work there. Visit nurseries that specialize in roses, where you'll probably get better information than at a garden center attached to a discount store. Read the specialty mail order catalogs, particularly from growers in your own horticultural zone.

Or, contact the American Rose Society to find a consulting rosarian close to where you live and ask them for recommendations for garden roses, rather than for the show roses.

In general, you should start off with something that is fragrant, doesn't get too big to handle easily, and blooms repeatedly throughout the growing season (nine months here in Dallas).

Once you discover how easy it is, you can begin to grow a wide variety. Roses can grow under some of the most difficult conditions imaginable. There is a piece of tall-grass prairie in Cedar Hill that has roses growing in it. They only get about 8 to 12 inches tall, and you can only find them when they are not blooming because when they are in flower, the prairie grasses are up and almost smother the little roses.

Choosing a wide variety of roses is generally a good idea because they all have different attributes. Some roses are resistant to one thing, others to another, so diversity increases the health of the entire garden.

What's the difference between a garden rose and a show rose?

The only difference is that there are some beautiful roses that require a little extra work to keep them going. The work is worth it if you plan to exhibit in a show or if you just like to have "perfect" roses in your garden.

But there are thousands of varieties (including many that can win prizes at a show) that may be well adapted to your garden, can settle in on their own roots, and live and flower for many years with normal garden maintenance.

If you choose roses that are suitable for your own growing conditions, have well-maintained organic soil, and a good mixture of other plants to provide a healthy environment for beneficial insects, roses become a joy rather than a job. Under these conditions, diseases such as black spot will be kept to a minimum, and unless you need absolutely perfect foliage for a rose show, you shouldn't need to spray with anything except foliar fertilizer.

Basically, just try any rose that attracts you. Plants respond differently to minute changes in growing conditions and a rose that does poorly in your neighbor's garden might grow bountifully in yours.

What exactly is an antique rose?

Rose terminology is very confusing. Roses have been a favorite garden plant for so long that there is a lot of lore and language attached to them. That is one reason it's useful to shop at specialty nurseries, where the staff has worked to learn about the world of roses.

The term "antique really

doesn't mean anything specific in reference to roses. It's more of a concept that includes all roses, ancient or modern, that have been around long enough to prove that they can perform well in ordinary garden conditions. When you see the word referring to a rose, however, you can be fairly certain that those plants have been selected for general health and hardiness and will do well for you.

I've heard anxious gardeners say they wanted antique roses because they are not hybrids—as if having a hybrid rose was an evil to be avoided. But all roses, except wild species roses, are hybrids due to the fact that they have two different parents. This does not mean they are any more difficult to grow than a species rose.

The term *Old Garden Rose* does have a strict historical definition. Old Garden Roses include all individual varieties belonging to any class (such as Tea, Bourbon, Noisette, China, etc.) that were already established when the first modern rose (a Hybrid Tea variety named 'La France') was introduced in 1867. Don't let it confuse you, though. Just choose a rose of any age that grows and blooms well for you.

If you buy a rose bush at a local department or discount store, will it be suited to your area?

It's hard to know because most of these are probably grafted onto a rootstock that has a broad range of acceptance, but your neighborhood or particular locale may not be included in that acceptance range. It might grow well in North Texas, but not in Central Texas, for example. If you can find a rose growing on its own rootstock and if it is a type that is adapted to your region, it should grow well.

What are the easiest roses to grow?

Most of the old Southern roses—the Noisettes, Teas, and Chinas—are almost bulletproof. Anyone can grow the Chinas, even if they think they can't grow anything. The more difficult roses to grow are the exhibition quality Floribundas, Hybrid Teas, and Hybrid Perpetuals. But, try anything you like because every inch of your garden is a separate universe. You might be able to grow a particular variety even if you have too much shade, or even if your neighbor can't grow it.

Do you have any suggestions for including roses in a garden design?

Although there are traditional ways of doing this, there are no hard-and-fast rules. You can choose a few roses to add to existing beds, plan your entire garden to complement the roses, or just keep a single bush in a whiskey barrel. It's up to you.

Southern gardeners seem to take pride in eccentricity, so if you're gardening in the South, there should be no limit to your creativity. Personally, I feel that all gardens should have lots of roses. You can squeeze a large number of roses into a relatively small place if you look at your garden as you would a fish tank—with bottom, middle, and top feeders. If you use every level of the tank you can keep more fish, all of them healthy. The same is true in the garden, which usually has sunlight available in underused places, particularly up high. You can have tiny roses as edging or drifts of color, medium to tall bushes as the blooming backbone, and climbing roses to reach up high and create a frame to envelop the entire garden space. Fill any empty spots with perennials, vegetables, herbs, whatever you like. You may have to settle occasional territorial disputes, but you'll probably never have to weed again.

ROSES FOR ALL LEVELS OF THE GARDEN

These older roses are easy to find and easy to grow, are repeat bloomers and are all fragrant, with the exception of the microminiatures.

Under 1 Foot
'Elfin Glow'—Mauve micro-
  miniature
'Si'—White microminiature
'Tiny Flame'—Coral micro-
  miniature

Under 2 Feet
'Beauty Secret'—Red miniature
'Lavender Lace'—Lavender
  miniature
'Nu Gold'—Yellow miniature
'Starina'—Orange/red miniature

2–4 Feet
'Hermosa'—Pink China
'Marie Pavié'—White Polyantha
'Martha Gonzales'—Red China
'Mrs. Oakley Fisher'—Apricot
  Hybrid Tea
'Oklahoma'—Dark red Hybrid
  Tea
'Souvenir de la Malmaison'—Pale
  pink Bourbon
'Sun Flare'—Yellow Floribunda

4–6 Feet
'Archduke Charles'—Red and
  pink China
'Duchesse de Brabant'—Pink Tea
'Iceberg'—White Floribunda
'Maggie'—Crimson Bourbon
'Mr. Lincoln'—Red Hybrid Tea
'Mrs. Pierre S. DuPont'—Yellow
  Hybrid Tea
'Thérèse Bugnet'—Deep pink
  Hybrid Rugosa

6+ Feet
'Altissimo'—Red Hybrid Tea
'Graham Thomas'—Dark yellow
  Shrub
'Mrs. B.R. Cant'—Silvery pink
  Tea
'Mutabilis'—Multicolored
  China
'Queen Elizabeth'—Coral pink
  Grandiflora
'Sally Holmes'—White Shrub
'Sarah Van Fleet'—Pink Hybrid
  Rugosa

Climbers/Pillar
'Belinda'—Deep pink Hybrid
  Musk
'Blossomtime'—Pink large-
  flowered Climber
'Buff Beauty'—Buff apricot
  Hybrid Musk
'Crépuscule'—Apricot orange
  Noisette
'Crimson Glory, Climbing'—Red
  Climbing Hybrid Tea
'Lamarque'—Lemon-white
  Noisette
'New Dawn'—Pale pink large-
  flowered Climber
'Perle des Jardins, Climbing'—
  Yellow Climbing Tea
'Red Fountain'—Red large-
  flowered Climber
'Sombreuil'—White Climbing
  Tea

ANNIE WEINREICH
Amarillo: Daylily Grower

Annie Weinreich grew up in a
family happily obsessed with
flowers, particularly daylilies.
Annie is actually a third-genera-
tion daylily grower. Her parents
were closely involved with a
Washington, D.C., daylily group,
and her father's mother was a
charter member of the American
Hemerocallis Society. When
Annie and her husband, Bill,
moved to their first home in
Pittsburgh, her parents gave
them a dozen tried and true
daylily varieties as a housewarm-
ing present—a gift that led to
Annie's own love of and involve-
ment with daylilies and the
Hemerocallis Society, including
serving as president in 1988 and
1989.

But Annie and Bill were not
able to enjoy their Pittsburgh
garden for very long.
"We moved around a
lot," Annie says, "but
we always had a garden
wherever we lived.
When we would have to
leave a place, we would
have what my dad called
'great plant giveaways.'
We would invite
gardening friends
to literally strip
the garden and

Daylily

take plants with them because we
were never convinced that who-
ever bought the house would
take care of the garden. But we
knew that friends, relatives, and
local garden club members would
love and appreciate the plants."

Annie finds it wonderfully
ironic that they now live in
Amarillo—a city that chose the
daylily as its floral emblem.

**How does growing daylilies
in Amarillo differ from growing daylilies in other parts of
Texas?**

In Houston or Dallas, you can
plant a newly hybridized seed at
the end of the season and a year
and a half later, you have a
bloom. In Amarillo, we have a
much shorter growing season
and the soil is difficult to work.
Even though the daylily has been
the city of Amarillo's floral
emblem for fifty years, it's still
not real easy to grow them here.

**What are the basic grow-
ing requirements for
daylilies?**

You need good, well-drained
garden soil, not anything really
special, just decent soil.
The pH preference is
a bit on the acidic
side, in the 6.0 to
6.5 range. The
plants need regular
watering and at least

six hours of full sun a day, prefer-
ably with a little shade in the late
afternoon. Other than that, they
don't need much. They will
grow most places in Texas with
nothing much more than an
application of Miracle Gro™.
They are virtually pest free.
Although aphids and spider mites
might deform the blooms, it
doesn't really hurt the plant.

**How many daylily varieties
are there?**

There are over 40,000 regis-
tered plants, dating back to 1897
when the first plant was regis-
tered. Many are no longer available, but we have fabulous newer
ones that represent a wealth of
variety. They vary from the plain
old roadside orange, *H. fulva*, to
some with 3-inch ruffled petals,
to some with big eyes or edges
of different colors. Some are 9
inches across, some only 2 inches. There are spidery daylilies
with long, narrow petals, and
some that are so double they
look almost like a peony.

**Which daylily varieties do
you recommend?**

You'll do best if you grow a
variety of daylilies because they
will complement each other. As
in a bouquet, each flower
enhances the one next to it.

**Why are daylilies so
popular?**

They are very easy to grow

and easy to hybridize. All you do
is take pollen from one plant and
put it onto the stigma of another
one and in a day or two the new
hybrid seed will begin forming.
It takes about forty-five days for
the seed pod to mature, then
they can be sown directly into
the soil, or potted up and put
into a greenhouse during winter
so the plants can be put outside
in spring. Some people refriger-
ate the seeds for a brief period to
trick them into going dormant
so that they will be ready to
plant as soon as it warms in
spring.

All the resulting flowers are
lovely, but some are more interesting or unusual than others. A
really great new cultivar will sell
for $100 to $200 a fan, but
it has to be quite unique to
demand a price like this. When
you have over 40,000 plants to
compete with, it's difficult.

**Are there goals for daylily
breeders?**

Even though there are blue
and white iris, these are two colors missing from daylilies, so
this is what people are working
toward. We have near-white and
cream, gold, yellow, perfect red,
salmon, pink, deep purple, and
brown but no blue and no white.
When that happens it will be a
wonderful addition to the garden, but in the meantime, you

can plant blue and white companion plants.

Does the foliage stay green all year?

There are some evergreen varieties that do well in the southern United States, but not in Amarillo. And there are some that go dormant and die back in winter; then there are some that are semi-evergreen, which is a halfway point. In Amarillo, the evergreen varieties do not do as well. The semi-evergreen and dormant varieties do fine. As for specific varieties, go to the

---

FAVORITE DAYLILIES

'Betty Woods'—Double yellow self
'Brocaded Gown'—Cream self
'Ed Murray'—Dark red self
'Gentle Shepherd'—Near-white self
'Mary Todd'—Yellow self
'Ruffled Apricot'—Apricot with pink midrib
'Seductor'—Red self
'Siloam Virginia Henson'—Pink with red eye
'Siloam Double Classic'—Double pink self
'Siloam Merle Kent'—Orchid with purple eye
'Stella D'Oro'—Miniature gold self
'Wind Falls'—Pink spider

---

experts in your area for information. If there is a Hemerocallis Society chapter, contact them, or go to a reputable garden and landscape store or botanical garden.

How do you plant daylilies if you order them through the mail?

You have to be careful, here in Texas, when you plant. You cannot plant bare roots (which is how they arrive when mail-ordered) during the summer if it is too hot. When the package arrives, take the bare roots out immediately, or as soon as possible, and put them into moist soil or vermiculite and wait until it gets cooler to plant them. If it's a good time to plant them directly into the garden, soak the roots for an hour or two to rejuvenate them first.

Be sure to space them 18 inches apart to allow room for growth. If you are growing several different kinds, make records of which varieties you are growing in each location.

How often do you have to divide daylilies?

You should dig and divide about every 5 to 6 years. The modern cultivars are not invasive like the old roadside orange, but they are hardy and you may need a knife or shovel to cut through them. But that tough hardiness is what makes them so good for a home landscape.

Dig up the entire plant and divide it, and then do not replant any piece larger than a clump of four fans. Don't divide or transplant daylilies in the heat of summer or too close to real cold weather because you want them to get re-established before they are stressed from extreme weather.

After you've replanted, you won't get much bloom the following year but each year after that you will get more and more flowers.

Do they need extra watering?

They appreciate extra water when they bloom. If you irrigate, they will have the best possible blooms. When cold weather comes, be sure to mulch them heavily.

When you replant, how deep should you put them?

Plant them as you would a new rose bush. Dig a hole and add lots of compost. Make a mound in the middle and place the junction of the leaves and roots no more than 1 inch below the soil level. Then put new, good, organic soil around the plant. If you plant too deeply, it will kill the plant faster than anything else. The natural tendency of a plant is to pull down deeper

into the soil and if it does that, it will never rise. Don't plant daylilies as shallowly as you would an iris, but be sure the crown is no more than 1 inch below the soil level.

Don't fertilize the first year, but after that, fertilize annually.

How do you know when to fertilize these plants?

It's very important, particularly here in the Panhandle of Texas, to have a soil test done with the county extension service. Our soils differ so greatly that each yard may need something different. In general, the application of a water soluble, balanced fertilizer is good. Most of our soils are high in phosphorous, which ties up the iron, so we have to be careful in adding manure because we don't want to add to the phosphorous level.

What do you add to increase the acidity?

Whatever works—bone meal, manure, leaf mulch. Anything organic will help.

What are some good companion plants for daylilies?

Short shasta daisies, spring bulbs, chrysanthemums, any kind of annual. Just be careful that you don't put in anything that will attract pests.

Do you have a favorite daylily?

I think 'Stella D'Oro' is

probably my favorite. The name means "star of gold" and it really has proven to be a star. 'Stella D'Oro' is a wonderful miniature yellow used commonly by landscapers. It has a greater number of blooms and a longer bloom time than almost any other variety. In some parts of Texas, you can even find this in bloom into November. It has brought awareness of daylilies to a lot of people who still thought that all daylilies were orange.

For more information, contact:

The American Hemerocallis Society
Pat Mercer, Executive Secretary
P.O. Box 10, Dexter, GA 31019
912-875-4110
gmercer@datastream.net

Resources

Sources for Naturalizing Narcissus

Old House Gardens
536 Third Street
Ann Arbor, MI 48103
734-995-1486

William R. P. Welch
P.O. Box 1736
Carmel Valley, CA 93924-1736
408-659-3830

McClure and Zimmerman
108 W. Winnebago
P.O. Box 368
Friesland, WI 53935
414-326-4220

The Daffodil Mart
7463 Heath Trail
Gloucester, VA 23061
800-255-2852

Display Gardens

See Appendix. Almost all public gardens in Texas have display beds showing perennials, annuals, roses, and bulbs.

Organizations

The American Hemerocallis Society
P.O. Box 10
Dexter, GA 31019
gmercer@datastream.net

The American Rose Society
Box 30,000
Shreveport, LA 71130
318-938-5402

Dallas Area Historical Rose Group
P.O. Box 38585
Dallas, TX 75238-0585

Heritage Rose Foundation
Charles A. Walker, Jr.
1512 Gorman Street
Raleigh, NC 27606
Send SASE for information

The Heritage Rose Group
100 Bear Oaks Drive
Martinez, CA 94553

Southern Garden History Society
Old Salem, Inc.
Drawer F Salem Station
Winston-Salem, NC 27108

The Texas Rose Rustlers
9426 Kerrwood
Houston, TX 77080-5428

Publications

BOOKS

Armitage, Allan. *Herbaceous Perennial Plants*. Athens, GA: GVarsity Press, 1989.

Beales, Peter. *Classic Roses*. New York: H. Holt and Co., 1985.

Bender, Steve and Felder Rushing. *Passalong Plants*. Chapel Hill, NC: UNC Press, 1993.

Brooklyn Botanic Garden. *Brooklyn Botanic Garden Easy Care Roses*.

Chapman, Lois Trigg. *The Southern Gardener's Book of Lists*. Dallas, TX: Taylor Publishing Company, 1994.

Culpeper, Elizabeth. *Heritage Roses and Old Fashioned Crafts*. Kangaroo Press, 1988.

Druitt, Liz and Michael Shoup. *Landscaping with Antique Roses*. Newtown, CT: Taunton Press, 1992.

Druitt, Liz. *The Organic Rose Garden*. Dallas, TX: Taylor Publishing, 1996.

Harper, Pamela and Frederick McGourty. *Perennials: How to Select, Grow, and Enjoy*. Los Angeles, CA: Price Stern Sloan, 1985.

Huber, Kathy and J. Lynn Peterson. *The Texas Flowerscaper: A Seasonal Guide to Bloom, Height, Color and Texture*. Salt Lake City, UT: Gibbs-Smith Publishing, 1995.

Lovejoy, Ann. *Further Along the Garden Path*. New York: Macmillan, 1995.

McKean, Judith. *Gardening With Roses*. Emmaus, PA: Rodale Press, 1995.

Miller, George O. and David Northington. *Landscaping With Native Plants of Texas and the Southwest*. Stillwater, MN: Voyageur Press, 1991.

Peters, Mike. *Texas Garden Almanac*. Missouri City, TX: MacMillen Publishing, LLC, 1998.

River Oaks Garden Club. *A Garden Book for Houston and the Texas Gulf Coast*. 1989.

Rougetel, Hazel. *Heritage Roses*. Owings Mill, MD: Stemmer House Publishing, Inc., 1995.

Scanniello, Stephen. *A Year of Roses*. New York: Henry Holt, 1997.

Scanniello, Stephen and Tania Bayard. *Climbing Roses*. New York: Prentice Hall, 1994.

Smith, Brenda Beust. *The Lazy Gardener's Guide, Upper Gulf Coast*. Houston, TX: River Bend Company, 1997.

Sperry, Neil. *Neil Sperry's Complete Guide to Texas Gardening*. Dallas, TX: Taylor Publishing Company, 1991.

———. *1001 Most Asked Texas Gardening Questions*. Ft. Worth, TX: Summit Publishing, 1997.

Squire, Sally McQueen. *The Complete Guide to Growing Bulbs in Houston*. Houston, TX: River Bend Company.

Sunset Southern Garden Book. Menlo Park, CA: Sunset Books, 1998.

Sunset Western Garden Book. Menlo Park, CA: Sunset Books, 1995.

Wasowski, Sally and Andy Wasowski. *Native Texas Gardens, Maximum Beauty, Minimum Upkeep*. Houston, TX: Gulf Publishing, 1997.

———. *Native Texas Plants: Landscaping Region by Region*. Houston, TX: Gulf Publishing, 1997.

Welch, William C. *Antique Roses for the South*. Dallas, TX: Taylor Publishing Company, 1990.

———. *Perennial Garden Color: Perennials, Cottage Gardens, Old Roses and Companion Plants*. Dallas, TX: Taylor Publishing Company, 1989.

MAGAZINES

Fine Gardening
Taunton Press
P.O. Box 355
63 South Main Street
Newtown, CT 06470

Flower and Garden
Modern Handcraft, Inc.
4251 Pennsylvania
Kansas City, MO 64111

Flower Gardening
Better Homes and Gardens
Special Interest Publications
1716 Locust Street
Des Moines, IA 50309-3697
512-284-3000

Horticulture
PO Box 2595
Boulder, CO 80323

Southern Living
PO Box 523
Birmingham, AL 35201

HERBS

MARIAN BUCHANAN
*Dallas: Herb Grower and
Educator*

Originally from the Rio Grande
Valley area, Marian Buchanan felt
as if she had moved to the frozen
northland when she and her husband settled in Dallas. But it was
in Dallas that she first discovered
a love of gardening. As her children grew older and demanded
less of her time, she cast about to
see what really interested her,
and it was gardening with herbs.
As the garden at her north Dallas
home grew and matured, she
began sharing it not only with
friends and family, but also with
school groups, senior citizens,
herb society members, and
anyone else who shared her
passion for green and growing things.

Marian's garden, which
she has shared now for about
ten years, is made up of two
distinctly different areas. The
first is a woodland, natural
garden where the careful selection of plant material and the
addition of water has resulted in
a successful wildlife habitat. The
other part of the backyard is a
more formal herb garden planted
in large raised beds, where children are encouraged to touch
and smell the myriad herbs
planted there.

Today, Marian shares not only
her garden, but her expertise as
well. She teaches a unit on herbs
in the Master Gardener program
and frequently visits nursing
homes and schools to tell people
about garden-
ing. She is
involved with
the Herb
Society of
America and
the Texas Herb
Growers and
Marketers and is
taking the first
Master Naturalist
course offered in North
Texas.

Basil

Is Dallas a good area for growing herbs?

It depends on which herbs you want to grow. The selection and positioning of plants is important. The plants that people are interested in don't always grow well here, but there are hundreds of herbs that will grow well if you treat them right—by amending the soil, for example. Plants that need acidic soils or a cool, moist root run aren't good choices. Our soils tend to be highly alkaline, compacted black clay, and our summers are long and sweltering. Our winters are subject to drastic fluctuations in temperatures. In this area, summer hardiness is as important as cold tolerance for growing plants.

How do you work with the soils for growing herbs?

Many herbs will tolerate a wide range of pH if they have the drainage they need. On un-amended soil, you're really best off growing plants native to our region, which have already adapted to our conditions. Many of the herbs that I grow are in raised beds or in mounded areas that are higher than the surrounding soil. I add generous amounts of organic matter to the soil, which helps to "open up" the clay soil, improves drainage, and makes nutrients more available to the plants.

Is humidity a problem?

It's not as bad here as it is on the Gulf Coast. We can grow more of the silver-leafed plants such as artemisia and some of the sages than they can in Houston, for example. But the herbs suffer from an occasional summer monsoon when the combination of heat and humidity will kill plants almost overnight.

We have two major planting seasons:
Fall: *Plant herbs such as thyme, oregano, parsley, cilantro, arugula, and chervil.*
Spring: *Plant more parsley and perennial herbs such as lavender, rosemary, thyme, and sage.*

When is the best time to plant herbs?

We have two major planting seasons, fall and spring (after the danger of frost has passed). In the fall, you can put in hardy perennials (thyme and oregano), cool season biennials (parsley), and cool season annuals (cilantro and chervil). I grow most of my cool season annuals and biennials from seed, including dill, cilantro, arugula, chervil, and parsley. With the exception of dill, these herbs stay green all winter. I also plant parsley in early spring because I want an abundance, both for the kitchen and for the butterflies. It's a great larval plant for swallowtail butterflies.

In late February, I plant more cilantro, arugula, and dill seeded directly into the garden. As the weather warms, these bolt and go to seed. I pull them up to make room for the basils, which I plant around May 1 because basil deteriorates when soil temperatures are lower than 50°. I simply press basil seeds into the ground and, if the soil is warm, they'll practically come up overnight.

Spring planting season for perennial herbs begins after the chance of freeze damage has passed, about mid-March in this area. This can mean a lot of hard work before the heat sets in. They should be planted early enough so that the young plants have a chance to become established before the heat sets in. Soil prep really needs to be done in the fall so that the ground will be ready and waiting for these young plants.

Are there ways to protect herbs from severe cold?

First, be sure that the plants are well established before cold weather comes. Don't plant too late in the fall and expect a young plant to do well when it's stressed by winter temperatures. Herbs that are marginally hardy, such as sweet marjoram, lemon verbena, and pineapple sage, may be covered with blankets or frost row covers, which are designed for this purpose, when a hard freeze is predicted. Never use plastic, as it can smother the plants. No matter what you use, the cover must be removed promptly before the morning sun can create a solar oven and bake the plants.

Don't harvest perennial herbs too late in the fall. Our average first freeze is around the first part of November. Cutting stimulates new growth that is susceptible to freeze damage. Don't forget that herbs may need occasional watering in winter if we have a long dry spell. Mulching helps, but don't layer the mulch against the stem or trunk of the plant where moisture can be trapped and rot the herb.

Do most of the herbs you grow need full sun?

There's a wide variety of herbs that don't need full sun in this part of the country. Many books say that they do, but these are books that were written in Connecticut or Great Britain and the authors have no idea of the intensity of our light and heat. Here, the majority of the herbs will be happy if they get half-day sun: morning sun and shade in the afternoon. Parsley, chervil, and several native herbs are natural understory plants, many of them with traditional medicinal uses. For example, our native mahonia was used as a blood purifier, sumac berries were used to treat bed wetting, and columbine seeds were used to control lice.

It sometimes seems that we were all born with an "overwatering gene." We tend to think that a sprinkle a day is good for everything, but it's better to soak plants thoroughly, then back off from watering and allow them to dry out thoroughly before you water again.

Some of the other herbs that I grow under large live oak trees include Solomon's seal, ginger, self-heal, black cohosh, hellebore, patchouli, and some salvias, such as *S. miniata, S. urica,* and *S. guaranitica.* Several of these herbs are toxic and should not be planted where children are playing unsupervised.

How about watering?

This is where I really get on my soapbox. It seems that we

were all born with an "overwatering gene." We tend to think that a sprinkle a day is good for everything. I tell people that a sprinkle a day is good for deodorant, but not so good for watering a plant. I hand-water the plants in the raised beds, soaking them thoroughly and then backing off and letting them dry out before watering again. Many people think that running a lawn sprinkler every other day will take care of the watering situation and they won't have to think about it. Not only is this inefficient and a waste of water, it is also an inappropriate way to water since it simply wets the top of the foliage and the very thin top layer of soil. If you water thoroughly, you help the plant create a complex root system that helps the plants withstand the stress of heat. You should really water with a soaker hose to a depth of 1 to 2 inches.

Of my eight formal planting beds, four are xeriscape beds which rarely, if ever, get supplemental watering. This is where I keep Mediterranean herbs such as rosemary, thyme, sage, oregano, lavender, and artemisias, which prefer to be dry and demand perfect drainage.

If you know the kind of ecosystem that a plant originally came from, then you'll have a better feel as to where to put it in your own garden. If you can put together plants that have similar environmental needs, such as full sun or abundant water, you'll be that much more efficient.

What are some of your favorite herbs?

I love the lavenders, but they are a challenge in our area. After they are established in my garden, though, I seldom have to water them again. I grow the English lavender 'Hidcote', 'Munstead', the pink-flowered 'Jean Davis', and a white 'Nana Alba'. I also grow French lavender (*L. dentata*) and Spanish lavender (*L. stoechas*), and some of the hybrids and cultivars such as 'Provence', 'Grosso', 'Silver Frost', and 'Croxton's Wild'. The French and Spanish lavenders seem to tolerate our humidity, although they are only marginally winter hardy. The English lavenders occasionally succumb to sudden wilts or fungal diseases that attack in the summer heat.

Another plant that I have just recently had success with is French tarragon. I generally do not recommend it because by July it's usually dead. It prefers winter dormancy, which our winters don't always supply. Last year I planted it under the roses and I remembered to water it

regularly. It seemed to like the little bit of shade it received from the rose bushes. I had huge mounds of it spilling out over the beds into the walks. It is growing in exactly the right spot in my garden. It needs good drainage and protection from the afternoon sun.

There are other herbs I've discovered that will flourish with good drainage and protection from the afternoon sun. Some of my favorites are scented geraniums and sweet bay, which do better as container plants that you can bring indoors since they are not reliably winter hardy. I put mints into containers, also, because they tend to be invasive. Other plants that benefit from protection from afternoon sun are onion chives, parsley, St. John's wort, comfrey, pineapple sage, and patchouli.

I usually just pick off bugs by hand. If a plant is terribly infected, I'll just dig it up and throw it away.

Are there herbs that grow well in containers?

Quite a few, but they require a little more time and attention than garden-grown plants. Herbs in containers are more vulnerable to the elements. The soil dries out faster, nutrients leach out faster, and heat and freezing temperatures can be more damaging. You need to check the moisture every day, and when you water, soak the root ball, keeping the foliage as dry as possible.

If freezing temperatures are forecast, bring pots of tender herbs indoors. Unless you have a greenhouse or very bright exposure from a window, though, most herbs are not happy with indoor growing conditions. If you can't move them or have no room for them indoors, wrap the pots with old carpeting or burlap and cover them if a hard freeze is predicted.

Some of the best herbs for containers include basil, chives, cilantro, dill, mints, oregano, parsley, rosemary, scented geraniums, and thyme. But just about any herb can be grown in a container as long as the pot is large enough to accommodate the root ball of the plant and the container drains properly. Instead of garden soil, use soilless potting mixtures, either store-bought or homemade.

Do you have problems with pests and diseases?

Not like you would with a vegetable garden. I never use synthetic pesticides and seldom use organic ones either. There are too many visitors in my garden, both young and old, and I want to be able to encourage them to nibble on the edible herbs without worrying about pesticide residue.

I usually just pick the bugs off by hand. If a plant is terribly infested, I'll just dig it up and throw it away. It's just not worth worrying about. Pests such as aphids, you can shoot off with a water hose or a soap spray.

Quite a few beneficial insects are attracted by the small flowers on many of my herbs and I'll often see ladybugs, lacewings, and predatory and parasitic wasps and flies in the garden. Birds, lizards, toads, and frogs also show up.

Pests such as aphids you can shoot off with a water hose or a soap spray.

I have a lot of caterpillars, but I just put up with the damage they do because I love the butterflies. I love it when a school group comes and I can show them all the creepy crawly things in the garden.

Diseased plants are usually the result of cultural problems that the gardener has contributed to, either by overwatering or not providing enough sun or air circulation.

Are there basic mistakes that you see people make in growing herbs in this area?

Not planning before they plant. People just don't take the time to prepare the soil correctly. Also, they tend not to think ahead. They impulse buy in the nurseries without finding out the cultural requirements of the dif-

HERBS FOR CONTAINERS	
Chives	*Allium schoenoprasum*
Bay	*Lauris nobilis*
Mint	*Mentha* sp.
Basil	*Ocimum* sp.
Oregano	*Origanum vulgare*
Scented geraniums	*Pelargonium* sp.
Rosemary	*Rosmarinus officinalis*
Thyme	*Thymus* sp.

HERBS TO GROW IN THE SHADE	
Columbine	*Aquilegia canadensis*
Gotu kola	*Centella asiatica*
Cohosh	*Cimicifuga racemosa*
Foxglove	*Digitalis purpurea*
Cardamom	*Elettaria cardamomum*
Hellebore	*Helleborus* sp.
Ginger	*Hexastylis* sp.
Mahonia	*Mahonia bealei*
Hoja santa	*Piper auritum*
Patchouli	*Pogostemen cablin*
Solomon's seal	*Polygonatum*
Self-heal	*Prunella vulgaris*
Salvia	*Salvia* sp.

ferent herbs and plants they are buying. They may or may not have the right place to put them when they get home.

They really need to do some research. Just because a plant is available in the nursery does not necessarily mean that it is appropriate for our area or that it is time to put it into the ground. I've seen basil in the stores in February and cilantro for sale in June, absolutely the wrong time to plant either one.

Many people are intimidated by the idea of growing herbs. They think that they are part of a mystical plant family that must have peculiar growing requirements. On one hand, it's easier than that, but on the other hand, it's more complicated because herbs represent all plant families from all over the world. People need to become acquainted with them on an individual basis and find out what they like, where they came from, and what they need.

Madalene Hill and Gwen Barclay
Round Top: International Festival Institute

Madalene Hill has always loved growing, cooking with, and sharing her knowledge of herbs. Through the years, her natural interest and undaunted enthusiasm for the subject has resulted in an astonishing knowledge of these plants. Not surprisingly, her daughter, Gwen, inherited—either through genes, environment, or both!—an interest in herb growing that eventually led her into the gardening and food service business. The combined efforts of these two women have led to many successful ventures, including restaurants, a book (*Southern Herb Growing*), and countless magazine and newspaper articles. Madalene has served as president of the American Herb Society; their fame has spread throughout the United States and beyond.

It began modestly enough, Madalene recalls. "We always grew food for our own use, and people were so interested in what we were doing that soon newspapers and TV were doing stories on us." Their home garden grew in size and fame, and in 1967, they opened a garden room restaurant that they created out of an old chicken house.

Today, this mother–daughter team calls the International Festival Institute in Round Top, Texas, their home. The Institute was established twenty-eight years ago by James Dick, a concert pianist who still serves as artistic director. His dream was to provide a summer institute, similar to those found throughout Europe, where young, talented musicians would have the opportunity for intensive study and important public performances. The highest purpose is focused on public education and

Rosemary

the training of young artists not only in fields such as music, drama, and ballet, but also in architecture, gardens, landscaping, and fine food.

At the Institute, Gwen serves as director of food services while Madalene spends her days tending the ever-growing herb gardens. The gardens consist of the wall gardens, which display antique roses, rosemaries, and herbs; the Cloister garden, which features herbs and flowers named for the Virgin Mary; and the Mediterranean garden, which showcases lavenders and other gray-leaved plants that are often difficult to grow in high humidity. The large terrace gardens contain herbs, including a large collection of rosemaries, annual and perennial herbs and flowers, roses, and small trees and shrubs.

The primary objectives of the gardens are the beautification of the grounds and the education of the public. Special activities centered around the garden include "herb days," workshops, forums, symposiums, and conferences held throughout the year.

How do I begin an herb garden if I've never gardened before?

Everything begins with the soil. Here at Festival Hill near Round Top, we grow many of

EASY BEGINNER HERBS	
Dill	*Anethum graveolens*
Chives	*Allium schoenoprasum*
Coriander	*Coriandrum sativum*
Basil	*Ocimum basilicum*
Oregano	*Origanum* sp.
Parsley	*Petroselinum crispum*
Rosemary	*Rosmarinus officinalis*
Sage	*Salvia* sp.
Thyme	*Thymus vulgaris*

our herbs in terraced beds, which we have built with topsoil, sterilized sheep manure, compost, and peat.

No matter what kind of soil you start with, you can almost always make it better with the addition of organic matter. This not only increases the nutrient value of the soil, but helps it drain better as well. Add whatever is available to you: compost, leaf mold, rotted manure—particularly sterilized sheep or steer manure—or cottonseed meal.

Do all herbs need full sun?

The old rule of thumb is six hours of direct sunlight for most herbs. Otherwise, the plants will not adequately develop the essential oils in the leaves and roots needed for culinary or medicinal use. Some herbs, such as lemon balm (*Melissa officinalis*), foxglove (*Digitalis purpurea*), pennyroyal (*Mentha pulegium*), violets (*Viola* sp.), sweet woodruff (*Galium odoratum*), and lady's mantle (*Alchemilla vulgaris*) will thrive in the shade.

At Festival Hill, we have some trees that give us early morning shade, so we try to group the herbs according to their sun requirements. For example, oreganos love full sun, so we place them together in a bed that receives all-day sun.

*T*ry to group herbs according to their sun requirements. For example, oreganos love full sun, so we place them together. Herbs such as lavender and thyme need good drainage and dry conditions, so we also group them together.

What are some of the easiest, most useful herbs for a beginner gardener?

I'd first try oregano (*Origanum* sp.), basil (*Ocimum basilicum*), thyme (*Thymus vulgaris*), rosemary (*Rosmarinus officinalis*), parsley (*Petroselinum crispum*), sage (*Salvia* sp.), chives (*Allium schoenoprasum*), coriander (*Coriandrum sativum*), and dill (*Anethum graveolens*).

Do you grow many different kinds of oreganos?

There are many different varieties and cultivars, and we keep them separated. They have different growing habits and different aromas and tastes. Some are very strong and not good for food at all, some have no fragrance, others smell delicious. The best for cooking include the Spanish oregano (*Origanum vulgare*), and the Greek oregano (*O. v.* var. 'Prismaticum'), and, best of all, *O.* × *majoricum*. The small-leafed varieties are also good, including *O. heracleoticum* and *O. onites*. All oreganos are hardy in Zones 6–9.

The best way to grow the oregano you want is to try a variety of them, then purchase a plant or cutting of those you want. Do not grow them from seed, as they cross-pollinate easily.

How about lavenders?

We grow many lavenders in our Mediterranean garden, where we have created a situation of excellent drainage. We use gravel as mulch. We put 2 to 3 inches of pea gravel around the plants, and we've had better luck with some of the gray-leaved Mediterranean herbs than we've ever had before.

What about rosemaries?

All rosemaries are either up-right or prostrate varieties, and both are classified as *Rosmarinus officinalis*. There are many varieties and cultivars available for each.

I've had a test program going on rosemaries since I found the variety 'Arp' in 1972. I was taken with it because it's so hardy. We now grow more than fifty varieties of rosemary, which are left in the ground here in Central Texas without any protection.

We sent 'Arp' up to Tom DeBaggio for him to test at the National Arboretum in Washington, D.C. He found one that had a different growth form, which he named 'Hill Hardy'. It grows as far north as Long Island without any protection at all, once it is established.

Another great rosemary is

GROWING TIPS

• Thyme likes well-drained soil and lots of sunshine.
• Keep basil watered, mulched, and the branches pinched back.
• For cold regions, try growing Rosemary 'Arp'.
• Use gravel as mulch when growing Mediterranean herbs such as rosemary, lavender, and thyme.

called 'Gorizia', named for Tom DeBaggio's ancestral home in Gorizia, Italy. It is a large rosemary and must be kept pruned. Just thin the outside branches, then shape it as you want it. 'Severn Sea' is from England and blooms much of the year. Here, at Festival Hill, the bees cover it even in January.

One of our newest rosemaries is called 'Rest Stop' because two ladies who drive here on a regular basis from Dallas took a cutting from this plant at a rest stop where they generally stop. It is a nice, big shrub.

'Blue Spire' has deep, deep blue flowers and 'Alba' has white blooms.

How are the different varieties of thyme classified?

They fall into three main groups: woody subshrubs, which grow 12 to 18 inches tall; creeping, which grows up to 6 inches tall; and flat creeper, growing only 1 to 2 inches tall. Each has its benefits. Although the flat creepers are difficult to harvest because the leaves are so small, they make wonderful ground covers and can also be used in containers.

The culinary thymes we use most often include the narrow-leaf French, the broadleaf English, and the green-leaved lemon thyme.

Like the other Mediterranean herbs, thyme likes well-drained soil and lots of sunshine.

Are there any special requirements for growing basil?

Basils, similar to other warm weather crops, like warm soil and warm air. It is very sensitive to the cold. There are an astonishing number of cultivars and varieties showing great variation in leaf and growth form. Some of them, such as bush basil (*Ocimum basilicum* 'Minimum Bush'), has small leaves and grows 12 to 18 inches tall. Others, such as 'Rubin', have deep purple ruffled leaves and a good flavor. 'Purple Ruffles' is nice, but tends to lose its color in the heat.

You can plant basil seeds directly into the garden when the soil has warmed in spring. Place the seeds on top of the soil and tamp down lightly to get them into good contact with the soil. Seeds germinate in a very short time, usually 3 to 6 days.

During the growing season, keep basil watered and mulched, and the branches pinched back to encourage bushy growth and retard the blooming process.

Over the years, have you seen fads or changes in the kinds of herbs people use?

Yes. When men came back from World War II, they remembered the herbs and seasoning in the Italian foods they had eaten and wanted something similar here.

During the 1960s, the herb of choice was oregano. The hippie generation helped the popularity of herbs, particularly culinary herbs, since there was such an emphasis on vegetarian foods.

During the eighties, everyone wanted to grow basil, and luckily almost anyone can grow this. During the early nineties, we've seen tremendous interest in cilantro with the growing popularity of ethnic foods.

Over the past 4 or 5 years, it seems to be medicinal herbs that are becoming popular as alternative medicines of all kinds are becoming more widespread.

Are there resources that we can turn to for accurate information about medicinal herbs?

If you have the time and patience, you can find out just about anything you need to know on the Internet. And Varro E. Tyler, Ph.D. has written a couple of excellent books called the *Honest Herbal* and *Herbs of Choice*.

Can you grow your own medicinal herbs?

Many gardeners want to use their own herbs out of their

gardens and some even have grand thoughts of making a lot of money growing herbs to sell to pharmaceutical companies. But what they don't understand is that it takes lots of plants to make a pound of something, and drug companies won't even talk to you unless you can produce a minimum of several hundred pounds of a useful herb.

Even for home use it's not always practical. For example, it takes several years to get an *Echinacea* plant with a big enough root to use and then you have to dig it up and destroy the plant.

However, there are many herbs that aren't strictly "medicinal" but are considered culinary with medicinal properties. These include chamomile, sage, oregano, basil, rosemary, parsley, catnip, and the mints. These won't cure serious illnesses, but they are good for things like a tummy ache.

Can herbs be used to treat something serious?

Yes, but there is so much more that we need to learn. Right now we don't know the side effects of using some of the herbs. Within a plant there may be a hundred different chemical constituencies. Some, such as those with an antibacterial or an antioxidant action, may be iden-

tified. There may be many that have not been identified, however. If you isolate that particular identified constituent and take only that, scientists know what will happen, but if you take a tea made from the entire plant, that may pose an entirely different situation.

Do different growing conditions affect the chemical makeup of the herb?

Yes. The amount of sun a plant receives, where it is grown, when it is harvested, the age of the plant, how it is dried and stored are all factors that influence the makeup of the plant.

LUCIA BETTLER
Houston: Lucia's Garden

Lucia Bettler believes in the healing properties of herbs, both from the medicinal value of the plant itself and in the incomparable joy and magic of growing and using these plants.

To this end, she and her husband, Michael, created Lucia's Garden, a wonderful store full of herbs and flowers and all conceivable paraphernalia associated with them. To walk into the store is to enter a place filled with the fragrance of potpourris and herbal cooking and the beauty of herbal wreaths and garlands.

Lucia is descended from a long line of Sicilian farmers and grew up in Houston, where her mother's garden was filled with fennel and mint. Inspired by a love of mythology and folklore, Lucia became interested in the history of herbs and food and used this knowledge to teach others about her favorite plants. Today she teaches classes on medicinal herbs, healing, cooking, and aromatherapy.

Floral wreath

How would you characterize the gardening climate for the Houston area?

Our frost-free growing season stretches from late February to mid-November, so we can grow a variety of things in great abundance. Gardening in Houston can be challenging, however. The summer heat and humidity is really tough on the plants and the rains in May and June can drown them. We've had good success, though, growing plants either in well-drained containers or raised beds that hold at least 9 inches of good growing soil.

What are some of the easiest herbs to grow in the Houston area?

There are many! Try basil (*Ocimum* sp.), burnet (*Sanguisorba* sp.), chives and garlic chives (*Allium schoenoprasum* and *A. tuberosum*), sweet fennel (*Foeniculum vulgare*), French sorrel (*Rumex acetosa*), and costmary (*Chrysanthemum balsamita*), which is also known as Bible leaf because people used to use the flat leaves as bookmarks in their Bibles.

We also have good luck with salvias, mints (*Mentha* sp.), several oregano varieties (*Origanum* sp.), lemon balm (*Melissa officinalis*), lemongrass (*Cymbopogon citratus*), lemon verbena (*Aloysia triphylla*), parsley (*Petroselinum crispum*), rosemary (*Rosemarinus officinalis*), cilantro (*Coriandrum sativum*), and dill (*Anethum graveolens*). The last two are winter herbs for us.

Do you use any chemicals in growing your herbs?

No, everything we do is organic. There are so many organic products out now that you really don't need to use chemicals on your garden. Organic fertilizers include named products such as GreenSense™, Earth Safe™, Maestro-Gro™,

GENERAL TIPS FOR HARVESTING HERBS

- Don't cut more than you think you can use immediately.
- Avoid harvesting on a rainy day unless you will use it that day.
- Don't prune more than one-third of the plant.
- Cut just above a leaf bud joint.
- Store cut herbs in a glass of water in the refrigerator for up to two days.
- Store cut herbs in damp paper towels or a plastic bag in the refrigerator for up to four days.
- Use 2–3 times more fresh herbs than dried.
- Add fresh herbs in the last 10–15 minutes of simmering dishes; the last 5 minutes of steamed vegetable dishes.

Manalfa™, and Ringer™, as well as generic materials such as alfalfa meal, bat guano, earthworm castings, seaweed, and fish emulsions.

For control of small insects such as aphids, we use liquid soap at 1 teaspoon per gallon of water. We also release ladybugs in spring and green lacewings in summer and fall for biological control. For slugs, snails, fleas, ticks, roaches, and chinch bugs we use beer traps and diatomaceous earth products mixed at a rate of 1 to 2 tablespoons per gallon of water, plus 1 tablespoon liquid soap.

How do you preserve the herbs you use for crafts and cooking?

I air dry whenever possible because I think this is the easiest method. I just put the plant material I want to dry out on a cookie sheet on top of the refrigerator or on the drain board. It takes just a few days to dry them this way if you strip the leaves off the stems. You can also dry little roses this way as well.

Many people hang the plants upside down, but I find that they get dusty drying this way. If you are serious about cooking with dried herbs, hang them upside down in bunches and put a paper bag over them to keep the dust off.

Are there some herbs that will not air dry well?

Instead of drying it, I generally make pesto from my basil. I add a little oregano and toasted pine nuts, put it into ice cube trays and have pesto all winter.

How else do you use basil?

The best way is to layer it with tomatoes and buffalo mozzarella and add a splash of herbal vinegar.

How do you make an herbal vinegar?

Our method is very simple. We don't heat the vinegar, and we don't set it out in the sun because it just gets too hot here in Houston. I take a clean gallon jar and fill it with vinegar and just stuff it with herbs such as sage, oregano, dill, rosemary, basil, parsley, thyme, or whatever I have in excess. I make a big batch of this, let it sit for two months in a dark spot, then decant it. To decant, pour the vinegar and herbs over a double

TIPS FOR HARVESTING
LEAF HERBS
• Harvest just before the plant comes into bloom, when oils are richest.
• Harvest between morning dew and beginning heat.
• Handle as little as possible to avoid bruising and releasing oils.
• Strip leaves off stems as soon as possible and set aside.
• Do not chop leaves until just before adding to food.
• Err on the light side; you can always add more herbs but you can't take them away.

layer of cheesecloth to strain it. Repeat this two or three times to get all the plant material out. At this point it is very rich and robust.

Then, I fill pretty bottles with the flavored vinegar, add fresh plant material for decorative purposes, then doll it up with a little raffia or dried flowers. It makes a great gift and is a good way to use up a lot of herbs at the end of the growing season.

What kind of vinegar do you begin with?

I usually use apple cider vinegar for a better flavor. I also use red or white wine vinegar or champagne or rice wine vinegar, depending on what color and flavor I want.

Do you make flavored oils as well?

If we make flavored oils, we use them immediately. We do not bottle it up because of the threat of botulism. The problem with botulism is that you can't see or smell it, yet it might be present in a bottle. It's just not worth the risk.

How do you make your own medicinal tinctures?

It's not difficult. You get a very clean, small jar and stuff it with fresh plant material. One of the herbs I like to use for tinctures is a wild plant, plantain

(*Plantago major*). After I pick it, I don't wash it with water. I just dust it off, then stuff the jar with it, and cover it with vodka. You could also use gin or brandy. I then use a chopstick to get all the air bubbles out. Cover it with a lid, plastic or metal.

Every few days I add a little more vodka to keep the bottle filled. Leave it in there for three weeks, then decant it, strain it, and put it in little stopper bottles. Plantain is used to treat bronchial conditions or phlegm.

Often, instead of taking the time to make them, I buy my tinctures from the wildcrafters.

Who are wildcrafters?

These are people who pick from the wild, where herbs are organic and powerful. I think herbs found in the wild are more potent. I learned from a man who studied with the Cherokee Indians that the closer to home a plant is grown, the better it is for you because it's in your medicine wheel. If you grow your own tomatoes, for example, they're best for you. But if you can't, then buy from someone near you, or at least in your own state. The farther you get away from your medicine wheel, the farther you get away from the energies you need to incorporate. That's why I take issue with eating food out of

season. People don't even know that apples are a fall crop anymore. Sometimes the only way I know when things are in season is by how the price fluctuates in the grocery store. You should really grow your own food, if at all possible. There's something rewarding and satisfying about sustaining yourself with things from the earth.

Do you use other herbs as medicines?

Herbs such as peppermint and chamomile are good for upset stomachs, but you have to be careful. Many people who are allergic to pollen will have a reaction to chamomile flowers, so you have to watch out. A parsley tincture can be taken as a general tonic. It is high in chlorophyll and vitamins A and C.

Lemon balm is said to "cheer the heart," and I sometimes take a few sprigs of lemon balm and one of mint in spring water.

Do you make oils to be used externally on the skin?

I sometimes make an oil infusion by taking a lot of plant material, such as comfrey, and macerating it, then pouring olive oil over it. After it sits about three weeks, decant it and use it as a rub-in massage. Comfrey oil is good for swollen feet and ankles. Do not take this internally, however. Calendula and plantain oils are good for softening the skin. A great foot massage oil could be made from combining all three of these plants.

Are there plants and herbs that could be dangerous if taken internally or used externally?

You should stay away from foxglove. Some people are so sensitive to it that even touching the leaf causes a reaction. Wormwood and other artemisias and pennyroyal, for example, should not be taken internally. There are many others.

You use some of these herbs in sleep pillows. What are these and how do you make them?

A sleep pillow is a small pillow filled with herbs that you put under your regular pillow. The scent from the herbs helps you sleep better. We usually use mugwort, lavender, hops, catnip, and rose petals—anything with a relaxing scent. To make a sleep pillow, simply take a small pillowcase or cloth bag and fill it with the dried herbs of your choice.

You use many of the dried herbs for making potpourris. How do you make potpourri and which herbs do you use?

To make potpourris you need to mix dried plant material, essential fragrant oils, and a fixative to help the scent last a long time. Some of the best essential oils include those made from bergamot, jasmine, lemon, lavender, musk, orange, patchouli, rose, sandalwood, violet, or verbena.

Fixatives include cinnamon bark or chips, cinnamon powder, cloves, orris root chips or powder, sandalwood chips, and tonka beans.

Some of the best potpourri flowers from your garden include anemones, ageratum, bachelor buttons, calendula, carnation, celosia, crape myrtle, geranium, hibiscus, hollyhock, hyacinth, lavender, marigold, pansy, rose, salvia, verbena, yarrow, and zinnia.

For a general recipe, choose plant material that will give you good color, texture, and aroma. Dry the plant material thoroughly, including seeds, spices, and fragrant leaves and petals of your choice. In a separate bowl, combine the fixative and the fragrance oils until all the oils are absorbed, then combine this with the dried plant material.

Stir well and place the mixture in an airtight container for 4 to 6 weeks, shaking or stirring it once a week.

I know that herbal teas and the planting of tea gardens are both gaining in popularity.

Which herbs and flowers are best for doing this?

Most of the lemon-scented herbs and mints make very good teas, as does pineapple sage and chamomile. The lemon herbs, like lemon balm and lemongrass, make excellent hot teas. Lemon verbena makes a wonderful lemony component for sweet cold tea.

To make tea, just put an abundance of fresh material into a teapot and pour boiling water over it. Let it steep for 3 to 5 minutes, depending on your taste, and enjoy.

Resources

Display Gardens

Blue Moon Gardens
Sharon Lee Smith and
Mary Wilhite
Rt. 2 Box 2190
Chandler, TX 75758
903-852-3897

Botanical Research Institute of
Texas
509 Pecan Street
Fort Worth, TX 76102-4060
1-817-332-4441
Great library, seventh largest herbarium in U.S., open to public.

Heritage Park
Along Trinity River on
Main Street
North of courthouse

Ft. Worth, TX 76102
Visitor's Bureau: 817-336-8791

Houston Garden Center
South Texas Unit of the
Herb Society of America
Herman Park
Houston, TX 77030
713-529-5371

International Festival Institute
P.O. Box 89
Round Top, TX 78954
409-249-3828

Lucia's Garden
2942 Virginia Street
Houston, TX 77098
713-523-6494

Mercer Arboretum and Botanic
Gardens
Aldine Westfield Road
Humble, TX 77338
281-443-8731

Moody Gardens
1 Hope Boulevard
Galveston, TX 77554

Our Family's Herbs and Such
Lana Sims
702 Llano
Pasadena, TX 77504-1527
713-943-1937

Stephen F. Austin University
Arboretum
Nacogdoches, TX 75962-3000
409-468-3705

Zilker Botanical Gardens
222 Barton Springs Road
Austin, TX 78746
512-477-8672

Organizations

American Herb Association
P.O. Box 1673
Nevada City, CA 95959-1673
916-265-9552

Herb Research Foundation
1007 Pearl Street, Suite 200
Boulder, CO 80302
303-449-2265

Herb Society of America, Inc.
9019 Kirtland Chardon Road
Mentor, OH 44094
440-256-0514

Publications

BOOKS

Adams, James. *Landscaping with Herbs*. Portland, OR: Timber Press, 1987.

Brown, Deni. *Herb Society of America's Encyclopedia of Herbs and Their Uses*. New York: Dorling Kindersley Publishers, 1995.

DeBaggio, Thomas and S. Belsinger. *Basil, An Herb Lover's Guide*. Loveland, CO: Interweave Press, 1996.

DeBaggio, Thomas. *Growing Herbs from Seed, Cutting and Root*. Loveland, CO: Interweave Press, 1994.

Hill, Madalene and Gwen Barclay. *Southern Herb Growing*. Fredericksburg, TX: Shearer Publishing, 1987.

Hutson, Lucinda. *The Herb Garden Cookbook*. Houston, TX: Gulf Publishing, 1992.

Meltzer, Sol. *Herb Gardening in Texas*. Houston, TX: Gulf Publishing, 1997.

Ohrbach, Barbara Milo. *The Scented Room*. New York: Clarkson N. Potter, Inc., 1990.

Rodale's Illustrated Encyclopedia of Herbs. Emmaus, PA: Rodale, 1987.

Simmons, Adelma Grenier. *Herb Gardening in Five Seasons*. New York: Hawthorne Books, 1964.

Tyler, Varro E. *The Honest Herbal*. Binghamton, NY: Haworth Press, 1993.

Tyler, Varro E. *Herbs of Choice*. Binghamton, NY: Haworth Press, 1993.

MAGAZINES

The Business of Herbs
439 Ponderosa Way
Jemez Springs, NM 87025-8025

Foster's Herb Business Bulletin
P.O. Box 454
Mount View, Arkansas 72560
501-368-7439

The Herb Companion
Interweave Press
201 E. Fourth Street
Loveland, CO 80537

The Herbal Connection
3343 Nolt Road
Lancaster, PA 17601-1507

The Herb Quarterly
H.Q. Press
P.O. Box 689
San Anselmo, CA 94979

The Herbalgram
The American Botanical Council
P.O. Box 201660
Austin, TX 78720-1660

Herban Lifestyles
84 Carpenter Road
New Hartford, CT 06057-3003

FRUITS AND VEGETABLES

BILL ADAMS AND
TOM LEROY
*Houston: Harris County
Extension Service*

For Bill Adams and Tom LeRoy, the love of gardening is second only to their love of sharing what they know about gardening. Both are extension agents for Harris County, near Houston, and both are knowledgeable about gardening in Texas and generous in their contributions to horticultural education.

Bill grew up in Oklahoma and received bachelor's and master's degrees in horticulture at Oklahoma State University. He developed an early love of gardening from his grandmother, whose "whole backyard was a garden, a mass of vegetables, poppies, roses, and bearded iris."

Tom, who received his degrees in horticulture and plant breeding at Texas A&M University, grew up in a non-gardening fam-ily and, by default, inherited all the yard work. He has taught classes in gardening and horticulture since 1976 and was instrumental in developing the Master Gardening Association in Harris County, which now has over 400 members.

Bill and Tom joined forces to write several books on gardening, which are invaluable, not only for Texas gardeners, but for gardeners throughout the Southeast. The first, *Vegetable Growing for Southern Gardens*, was followed by *Growing Fruits and Nuts in the South* and *Commonsense Vegetable Gardening for the South*.

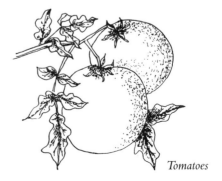

Tomatoes

How have you seen the interest in gardening grow over the past ten years?

Public interest in gardening has increased dramatically. There is not only great interest in home gardens, there also seems to be a great interest in market gardens—a small-acreage garden where specialty crops are grown. People are interested in growing cut flowers, herbs, fruits, or gourmet vegetables to sell to local florists, restaurants, or gourmet grocers.

Part of what we do here at the Harris County Extension office is to put in test beds to look at different varieties and determine which ones are best suited for our area. Many of the plants that people have grown for a long time are not the best ones for this area, so we are trying to find better varieties for us.

How important is it to choose varieties suited to your own locale?

We feel that it's very important. For example, you might have a peach variety that only grows well in a 30- or 40-mile area and won't grow well anywhere else in the state. Other varieties, such as some of the pears, will grow and thrive anywhere. As a general rule, localized varieties will grow better,

but some crops are more adaptable than others.

That is one reason why we write books. We have tested so many different varieties that we wanted to pass on the results. We feel that our books are as useful to Southern gardeners as a hoe or a rake.

Do some local nurseries still sell varieties that simply won't grow in your area?

Yes, and much of this has to do with name recognition of some of these varieties. For example, everyone knows 'Bartlett' pear, so that's what many nurseries carry, even though that particular variety will not grow anywhere in Texas, except perhaps the Panhandle. And they sell 'Thompson' seedless grape, but that is not a variety suited to growing in Texas.

What are the different growing regions in Texas?

We have five different USDA horticultural zones in Texas—all the way from tropical Zone 9 in the south to Zone 5 in the Panhandle. In Texas, you can grow everything from bananas to blue spruce. Along the Gulf Coast, you have high humidity and high rainfall—up to 45 inches a year in some areas. South of Houston, we have less rainfall but still have high humidity.

What's really surprising about growing regions in Texas is how rapidly they change, particularly along the coast. Climatic changes occur every 10 miles when you're within 50 miles of the coast. That means that what people are growing in Kemah, 40 miles southeast of Houston, is quite different from what we can grow here.

What are the soils like in Harris County?

They differ greatly, and the city of Houston seems to be the dividing line. In the eastern part of the county, you have sandy, acid soils with lots of pine trees. It's a good area to grow blueberries. On the southwest side of the county, you have clay soils that would never support blueberries. You can grow muscadine grapes in the western part of the county, but not much farther west than this.

It's not just a single factor that determines what you can or cannot grow in this part of Texas, but many different things. One of the tricks of gardening here is locating microclimates on your site and finding crops and plants that will grow in the sites you have available.

When is the best time to plant a garden in the Houston area?

We actually have four growing seasons here—two cool and two warm seasons. I think in this area, the winter garden is our best garden. From September until May is a wonderful time to garden and is a time that, unfortunately, most people don't think about gardening. Too many gardeners only think about gardening in spring and summer.

We can plant cool-season crops at the beginning of cool weather and the end of really cold weather—in September and October and again in January. Some of the quick-growing crops, such as radishes, we can plant once a month all winter.

Warm-season plantings are done in late February and March and again in July and August, when we still have enough time to get a crop in before cold weather.

We really encourage people to

COOL-WEATHER CROPS	
Broccoli	Spinach
Garlic	Lettuce
Cauliflower	Leeks
Chinese cabbage	Endive
	Celery
Radish	Mustard
Beets	Collards
Carrots	Turnips

use a fiber row covering, which helps protect the crops. This is a lightweight fabric that allows sun, light, and moisture through but protects the plants from temperature extremes. We use it in fall to protect from lingering heat and in spring to protect against late frosts and cold temperatures.

What kinds of crops would you put into a fall garden?

Cool-weather crops include broccoli, cauliflower, garlic, cabbage, Chinese cabbage, radishes, beets, and carrots. It's also the best time to plant greens and salad crops such as spinach, lettuce, leeks, endive, celery, mustard, collards, and turnips.

If I've never planted a vegetable garden before, how do I get started?

We suggest that people put in raised beds, whether you plant in a box or just raise the soil level where you are going to plant. This way you can bring in good soil, mixed with lots and lots of organic matter. In Harris County, many of the soils are heavy clay and it's hard for people to do enough work to make it plantable and productive.

We've found that the best thing you can do is forget about the soil you have, bring in good soil and begin with that. Raised beds also help with drainage. We

get between 45 and 60 inches of rain a year. Often, it comes all at one time and if you don't have raised beds, the soil all floats off. The beds should be at least 8 inches deep—12 inches is preferable.

Sometimes you can achieve this by working the soil into ridges in the garden and planting high on the ridges. If you have a big garden and use a tiller, there are attachments available to form these ridges. But again, how you plant depends on where you live. For example, in El Paso where water is scarce, they might plant in the valleys between the ridges.

In the Houston area, the winter garden is our best garden. From September to May is a wonderful time to garden. We can plant the cool-season crops at the beginning of cool weather, in September or October, and again at the end of the really cold weather, in late January.

If you bring in soil, is it still important to have a soil test done? What do you add to the soils to increase fertility?

It's probably more important because you don't know where

the soil has come from. It's important to know what's in your soil so you can amend it in the right way. Most regular gardening books will tell you to add phosphorous to the soil, but many of our soils are naturally high in phosphorous and adding more would be a big mistake. The standard recommendation for fertilizer in the vegetable garden used to be 12-24-12, but now we are recommending 15-5-10 or something such as potassium nitrate or cottonseed meal that has no phosphorous in it.

What happens if the phosphorous level is too high?

It ties up the iron and the result will be stunted growth and chlorotic yellowing, all signs of lack of iron.

Are heirloom vegetables more durable for this climate?

Many people push heirloom varieties because they believe they are hardier, but actually what we've found is that you're better off using newer hybrids that are more disease resistant and vigorous and grow faster. In taste tests, it's been found that people actually prefer the taste of most of the newer hybrids over that of the heirloom vegetables.

For example, not only do most people prefer the taste of hybrid tomatoes, they usually get much more fruit from these

plants as well. We've tested many different varieties and have found that the older varieties just don't produce as heavily. Some heirloom varieties will produce 4 to 5 pounds of fruit, whereas some of the newer hybrids will produce 40 to 50 pounds of fruit per plant.

What are some of the best tomato varieties that you've found for the Houston area?

We test about twenty-five varieties each year . Some of our favorite are 'Champion', 'Celebrity', 'Donna', 'Carmelo', 'French', 'Sweet Chelsea', and 'Baxter Early', which produced 76 pounds of tomatoes on one plant. All of these can be grown commercially as well as in a home garden.

FAVORITE TOMATO VARIETIES

Champion
Celebrity
Donna
Carmelo
French
Sweet Chelsea
Baxter Early

When do you plant tomatoes in the Houston area?

In early March we transplant 1-gallon plants into the garden. We suggest that the average gardener buy plants rather than trying to grow from seed. Most garden centers carry a good selection of tomato varieties.

We also tell people that if they are only putting in a half dozen or so plants to go ahead and put them out in mid-February. If they freeze, buy six more. If you can get them started early, you have a big advantage. Even if the soil hasn't warmed, it doesn't matter because tomatoes will grow in cool soils. With tomatoes, if you miss the best planting window even by a week, you miss a lot of production. Our last freeze date averages around February 20. Half the time you might get caught by a late freeze, but then half the time you won't. One year we had to plant three times, but we think it's worth the risk of planting early to get a good start on the season.

What method do you recommend when planting tomatoes?

First, work with the soil and put in fertilizer such as 15-5-10 that is high in nitrogen, such as calcium nitrate, cottonseed meal, or potassium nitrate. Then, put 2 tablespoons slow release fertilizer, such as Osmocote™, in the hole with each plant.

If the plants are long and leggy, we lay them on their sides. If they are good, stocky plants, this is not necessary. Then we cage them and wrap row cover around the cages, using clothespins or staples to hold the row cover. After they're up 18 to 24 inches or so, remove 2 or 3 sets of lower leaves to ensure good air circulation. We give the plants a foliar application of liquid fertilizer, such as Miracle Gro™, on a weekly basis right from the beginning, just spraying right through the row cover. That way we get about 50 pounds of fruit per plant. If they grow out of the cage, we try to keep them pinched back, but eventually we lose control and they go crazy. Generally we can carry plants into late July, but then we pull them up because they suffer from the heat and get spider mites and other insects.

Do you put in two crops of tomatoes or just one?

We haven't had much luck with fall tomatoes except for an old variety called 'Porters', which is a small-fruited variety that Bill's grandmother used to plant. It has little pink, plum-shaped fruits with an adequate flavor. We had a tremendous crop last fall. We put them in in July and put row covers over to protect it from the heat. It was too hot to set flower or fruit, but not too hot to grow. We had a plant big enough to produce when the weather cooled.

Why do fall tomatoes seem to stay green so long?

Fruit matures more slowly as the days get shorter and cooler.

Can you pick tomatoes green?

Yes, even though the flavor will not be as good as those that ripen on the vine. But you can either use them green to make relish or fried green tomatoes, or you can allow them to ripen indoors. Tomatoes should never go into the refrigerator, though. That's the kiss of death for flavor. The tomatoes you buy from the grocery taste lousy anyway, so putting them in the refrigerator is not going to make much difference.

What are some other popular crops?

Okra is popular. Most varieties are very localized, but some can be grown in many places. One of the more adaptable is 'Cajun Delight', which is a heavy producer. You have to pick the fruit when it's small, though. If you let it get longer than 2 inches long, it will be as tough as wood. 'Gold Coast' has a unique flavor but seems to take on the identity of whatever you are cooking with it.

People love to grow bell peppers as well, but they need soil that is so high in fertility you almost burn the plant with fertilizer.

What kinds of fertilizers do you use?

Any of the commercially available fertilizers such as Miracle Gro™, Rapid Grow™, or Peters™ all work fine. For most vegetables, you can get by with feeding every 3 to 4 weeks. If you're using a slow-release fertilizer, feed about every 6 to 8 weeks and use a foliar fertilizer weekly. If you have 1,600 square feet of garden beds, it takes about a half hour a week to foliar feed.

Are there general pests and diseases you're faced with every year?

Yes, but we encourage people to use a commonsense approach to the use of pesticides. We try to spray as little as possible, but we won't give up a crop to stink bugs or spider mites. If you catch the problem early on, you can usually use high-pressure sprays or simply pick off the pests.

If a home owner has to use a pesticide, he needs to do so with common sense. If the label says to wait two weeks after application before harvest, then he needs to wait. Few pesticides are systemic. Most are superficial and they can be washed off, although you still have to follow the directions on the label at harvest time.

Are chemicals generic for vegetable gardens?

No, they are becoming more

and more specific. You need to know enough about the problem to identify the correct cure before you do anything. People used to see an insect on a garden plant and grab the first spray they could find. Many insects may or may not hurt vegetables. Some pests, such as leaf miners or cucumber beetles, just don't do enough damage to worry about. Many things you just need to learn to live with.

Are there any other bits of advice you would give to a beginning gardener?

Work with the soil. It's hard work, but the soil should get better every year. Also, don't start off too large. Get comfortable with a small space and then grow gradually. Many people don't realize the amount of time and work it takes to garden.

Also, just grow what you're going to use or give away. If you don't eat parsnips, don't plant them.

JULIAN SAULS
Weslaco: Texas A&M University Extension Service

Professor and extension horticulturist for Texas A&M at Weslaco, Julian Sauls was born in Mississippi and grew up in Louisiana. Because was raised in a family that always farmed, and

he spent long hours as a youngster in the field picking and hoeing cotton and doing other farm chores, he thought that he would never have anything to do with growing or hoeing or picking again. But a love of plants and an interest in agriculture took him to Louisiana State University, where he earned both bachelor's and master's degrees in horticulture, and on to the University of Florida where he received a doctorate degree in horticulture, with a focus on fruit crops.

Luckily for the state of Texas, Julian then moved to Weslaco to work with the Texas Agricultural Extension Service, where he turned his time and energies toward raising citrus. His knowledge and expertise in this field has proven to be invaluable both for commercial growers and for home gardeners throughout the area.

Grapefruit

How do you compare growing citrus in Florida and in Texas?

In rains a lot in Florida and the soils are generally sandy. Here, in the Rio Grande Valley, the average rainfall is 24 inches. Our climate is drier and warmer than citrus growing regions in Florida.

How would you delineate the regions of Texas where you can safely grow citrus?

I use Highway 90 as a break line. That runs from Del Rio to Orange, and anywhere south of that, with precautions and care, you can grow some subtropical fruits in most years. There are basically four counties within the lower Rio Grande valley that have large commercial orchards: Starr, Hidalgo, Cameron, and Willacy.

At one time there was a sizable citrus industry in Carrizo Springs, but hard freezes in '83 and '85 and '89 knocked this down to nearly nothing.

What are your soils like in this area and do you have to amend them to grow citrus?

The soils here are alkaline to moderately alkaline but we do little to adjust the pH. Citrus prefers a pH range from 6.0 to 8.0 but seems to be well adapted to our soils. Soil amendments are not usually added, simply because they are not readily available here. In East Texas you have leaves, wood chips, shavings, and other by-products of the forest industry, but there aren't trees or forest products here so there's nothing easily attainable to use as mulch or soil amendment.

Good drainage is more critical than adding things to the soil. Citrus trees need deep soils that drain well. If you're not certain if your soil drains well, look at the landscape trees close by. If they look lush and healthy, chances are the soil is deep and well-drained enough to grow citrus as well.

A big mistake people make in planting citrus trees is to simply remove turf grass and create a basin four to six feet in diameter. If you plant a tree in the middle of this sunken basin, the bud union is three to six inches below the soil line. This might be good conditions for a live oak tree, but it's a death knell for citrus. Like clockwork, four to five years after planting, these trees get root rot and die.

Is the salinity of the soil and water a problem?

It could be, but right now it is not a major factor. We get two rainy periods—first in May and June, and then again in September—so we usually get enough rainfall to get general leaching of the soil. The river water salinity is probably 800–1000 parts per million, which is higher than we'd like but lower than it could be. For things like citrus, the impact of salinity is imperceptible. Crops such as avocado or pecans would show necrosis in July and August.

What other factors should you consider when you are putting in citrus trees?

Citrus trees need full sun to grow and produce well, so be sure to plant them in a sunny area. Try not to plant near a septic tank, just to avoid problems with the roots clogging the lines in years to come. And be sure to site them in areas where they will have plenty of room to grow. Plant the trees at least 6 to 8 feet from a structure or driveway, and 12 to 14 feet from one another.

If I were a home owner new to the region and wanted to grow citrus, what varieties would you recommend I start with?

Most of the varieties sold at local garden centers or nurseries are adapted to our region. Many of these are grafted onto sour orange rootstock and perform well in our soils. Trifoliate orange rootstock is also used and this produces a smaller tree that

is more cold hardy. Unfortunately, it is not adapted to our alkaline, salty soils, so we do not use it here. It is the preferred rootstock for the upper Gulf Coast and colder areas, however. Because of citrus quarantine, we can't bring in trees from other citrus states such as Florida, California, or Arizona, so all our trees are locally grown.

The Texas Agricultural Extension Service has worked hard over the years to collaborate with the nursery industry so that the varieties offered in gardening stores are varieties that will grow best in each region. This is not always true of the discount chains that generally have national corporate buyers.

Are there new varieties of citrus being developed?

Not really. The commercially available grapefruit and oranges are not varieties that originated from a classical plant breeding program. They were, instead, the result of chance mutations. For example, Texas is the home of the red grapefruit because it was first discovered and developed here. In the twenties and thirties there were many of these mutations. People want to know why, what was different about the twenties and thirties? I don't think that anything was different except the way that people

CITRUS FOR
SOUTH TEXAS

Sweet orange—'Marrs',
'Navel', 'Valencia',
'Pineapple'
Grapefruit—'Rio Red' or
'Ruby Red'
Limes—'Mexican'
Lemons—'Meyers' (also
known as valley lemon),
'Ponderosa'

worked their orchards. In earlier times, the men and women who owned these orchards weren't driving through in air-conditioned trucks. They were walking through and seeing the trees more closely, picking some of the fruit themselves. When you're doing that, you're more likely to spot something different or unusual.

Are there precautions that home growers can take to protect against cold weather?

Site selection is important. Since all the cold weather arrives from the northwest, plant the trees on the southeast side of the house, if you can. The house itself will offer some protection because there is radiant heat loss from an occupied structure. Soil banks—mounds of dirt piled as high as you can around the trunk and lower limbs—are useful for

young trees from Thanksgiving until about the first of March. Just be careful when you're taking the soil bank down in spring.

Temporary covers such as blankets, quilts, or tarps are useful during a hard freeze, as is temporary supplemental heat from a Coleman™ lantern or an incandescent lightbulb.

What is the best method of actually planting a citrus tree?

The biggest problems we have are with container-grown trees because people don't know how to plant correctly. These trees are grown in an artificial medium without soil. That organic medium is great for growing in a nursery setting where the plants are watered daily and fertilized weekly, but when people get home with these plants they simply plop them into the ground and nothing happens. The problem is that there is an interface established between the artificial growth medium and the real-world

PROTECTION AGAINST
COLD

• Good site selection
• Dirt mounds around trunk and lower limbs
• Temporary covers (blanket, quilt, tarp) for unusually cold temperatures

soil, and it's difficult for water and air to move across this. As a consequence, the roots of a container-grown tree tend to stay right in the same tight ball that it started out in.

We found that if you take the garden hose and wash off 1 to 2 inches of this soilless medium all around and on the top to expose the outer reaches of the roots and then plant the tree, the outer perimeter of the roots is in direct contact with the real-world soil and they'll take off and start growing. You don't need to mix topsoil, compost, or anything else with the backfill soil.

What's the best time to plant?

Whenever you can get them in. You can really plant twelve months out of the year. Ideally, you want to plant in September and October, which will give you the cooler months and shorter days to allow the plant to become established before the stress of late spring and summer.

How much water is required?

You cannot grow citrus here without supplemental water—24 inches annually is simply not enough. Citrus needs about 50 inches per year. In February and March, and again in September and October, you'll need about an inch per week. During the

> ### GOOD GROWING CONDITIONS FOR CITRUS
> - Full sun
> - Plenty of room to grow:
>   - At least 6–8 feet from a structure or driveway
>   - 12–14 feet from one another
>   - Away from a septic tank
> - Deep, well-drained soils
> - Ideal pH 6.0–8.0

warmer months, when transpiration is higher, you might want to kick it up to 1 1/2 inches per week.

Newly planted trees will need to be thoroughly watered 2 or 3 times the first week and once or twice a week for the next few weeks until they are well established.

How about fertilizers?

The only fertilization necessary is nitrogen. You should not fertilize young trees until new growth appears, then fertilize once a month, through October. The best way to do this is to scatter fertilizer in a circle at least 1 foot away from the tree trunk, then water thoroughly.

What about other care—weeding, pruning, pest control?

Controlling grasses and weeds that compete with the young

trees is important. Especially when the trees have been planted in a lawn area, you have to keep the grass a couple of feet away from the tree.

A citrus tree that has been properly shaped at the nursery should not need pruning.

The pests we have are not life-threatening. Things such as blackflies, whiteflies, aphids, leaf miners, rust mites, and citrus mites all affect the fruit, but unless gardeners are trying to grow show quality, blemish-free fruit, these will not really hurt the tree severely. We recommend that home owners grow citrus organically because the correct use of chemicals requires a good bit of education. Spraying incorrectly can do more harm than good.

Can citrus be grown in containers as well as in the ground?

Yes, especially smaller types such as lime, kumquat, lemon, and calamondin. The size of the container is the greatest limiting factor—it has to be big enough to allow for good growth, but small enough to move easily during freezing weather. Be careful not to overwater, as this is the most common problem with container-grown plants. Allow the top inch of the potting medium to dry out before watering again.

JERRY PARSONS
San Antonio: Bexar County Extension Service

Originally from Somerville, Tennessee, Texas Extension Horticulturist Jerry Parsons has retained a Southern drawl that delights the folks with whom he works in Bexar County. But it isn't just the accent that people like, it's the expert advice, generously sprinkled with a wonderful sense of humor, that keeps Jerry's phone ringing.

Although his family raised cotton, corn, soybeans, and cattle, they "knew little about horticultural crops such as flowers and garden vegetables," Jerry admits. But influenced and encouraged by a great-uncle who raised tomatoes and "loved to eat what he raised," Jerry set his educational sights on a career in horticulture.

Jerry earned a bachelor's degree at the University of Tennessee, a master's degree at Mississippi State, and a Ph.D. at Kansas State University, where he specialized in horticulture with a focus on fruit crops.

In 1974, he moved to the winter garden area of Texas, where 25 million dollars' worth of vegetables are produced annually. Today, as Extension Horticulturist, Jerry works

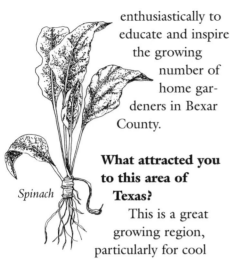

Spinach

enthusiastically to educate and inspire the growing number of home gardeners in Bexar County.

What attracted you to this area of Texas?

This is a great growing region, particularly for cool weather crops such as cabbage, carrots, and spinach. Fifty percent of all the spinach grown in the United States is grown within 100 miles of San Antonio.

How are growing conditions here different from other places you have been?

In San Antonio, the soil pH ranges from 7.8 to 8.2, and plants that prefer acidic soils, such as azaleas and blueberries, won't grow here. Vegetables, however, seem to be ideally suited to these soils. Some varieties might get iron chlorosis, but we're constantly testing to see which crops and varieties perform well here.

We do have extreme fluctuations in temperature. It can be mild, in the seventies and eighties in December, and then all of a sudden it can drop to twenty-five degrees. Plants do not have a chance to harden off. That's why

the cold kills so many plants. This is not as critical with vegetables that you grow as annuals as it is with trees or perennials.

Are there vegetable crops that are more susceptible to damage from cold than others?

Head lettuce is easily damaged. Most of the lettuce grown in the U.S. is grown in California or Florida. If you look at a planting zone map, you'll see that we're all in the same zone, yet we can't grow lettuce because of our fluctuating temperatures. If you're a wise gardener here, you'll plant for things recommended two zones higher than you are.

If you are a wise gardener here, you'll plant things recommended for two zones higher than you are. We can't grow many things that other people in our zone grow because we have such widely fluctuating temperatures.

What are your planting dates?

In San Antonio, the average first frost is November 15 and the last is March 15. These are different from the "farmer dates" that the old-timers go by. The official weather department bases its official frost dates on averages. Well, if you stand with one foot in boiling water and the other foot in ice water, you're on the average comfortable. We go to such extremes from year to year that there's no such thing as an average year.

Also, you have to remember that within 40 miles of downtown San Antonio, you move into a different planting zone. When you go south, the last frost date is in February, but in the hill country, north, it is in April. It's best to contact your local extension service office to find out the specific planting times for your area.

Are there ways to protect plants from a hard freeze?

One of the best ways is to use spun web frost row cover. If you put that over the plant, it gives some protection from wind, hail, and insects, and gives you a 4-degree temperature buffer. The temperatures can go down to 30°, but if you have this over your plants, they should be okay. You can put this over the crops when you plant them and just leave it on because it allows sunlight through it. Wrapped around a wire structure such as a tomato cage, it makes a little cloche or igloo for the plants and makes a lot of sense. When you wrap the cage with it, attach it with clothespins and water straight through it, being sure to water around the roots and not wet the foliage.

The problem is, people won't use it because they can't see the vegetables and people want to see what they're growing. I tell them it's better not to see a vegetable because it's covered up than to see one dead from cold weather, hail, or bugs.

One of the best ways to protect against frost is to use spun web frost row cover. It gives you some protection from wind, hail, and insects, and gives you a 4-degree temperature buffer.

Is it important to water before cold weather comes?

Yes. Any plant going into a stressful period benefits from extra water. We can get a dry winter and people won't water anything because they think the plants are dead, but usually the plants aren't dead, they're just sleeping.

When do you plant spinach here?

In San Antonio we put it in in

October. Spinach is fairly slow to germinate and is difficult to grow from seed, so we have convinced growers to supply the nurseries with new, disease-resistant varieties of spinach transplants. You can put these transplants in from October to January or February. Spinach does extremely well in our alkaline soils. It's a great plant—dark green, high in vitamin A, and one of the most nutritious vegetables.

We don't do as well with lettuce because we don't have the cool nights to develop the sweetness.

At this same time, you can plant other cool-weather crops such as radishes, turnips, broccoli, cauliflower, and carrots. We can garden ten months out of the year—every month except July and January.

The numbers on a bag of fertilizer indicate levels of nitrogen (N), phosphorous (P), and potassium (K), and are always listed in this order.

Do you have advice for home owners who want to grow summer crops such as tomatoes and peppers?

Plant as close to the last frost date as possible—mid-March in San Antonio. Be sure that you prepare your soil well. Vegetables like a rich soil high in organic matter, so add a lot of compost. You can also add manure, although different types vary greatly in nutritional makeup, depending on the kind you use and how much it has aged. For sheep, rabbit, or cow manure, we recommend 50 pounds per 100 square feet or 10 tons an acre. You need to mix this into the top 8 to 12 inches of soil.

For tomatoes, you should use transplants that are 4 to 5 weeks old, growing in 4-inch peat pots. For caged tomatoes, they should be spaced 3 feet apart, although smaller varieties such as 'Surefire' can be planted as close as 2 feet apart. If your transplants are leggy, set them on their sides rather than planting them deeper. This will help the plant develop a better root system. You can't do this with peppers, however, for the stem will rot.

Once the soil temperature has reached 70°, put a layer of mulch around the plant but not touching the stem. The mulch helps conserve soil moisture and maintain an even soil temperature. You can use a variety of materials for mulch, including clean wheat straw, rye straw, alfalfa, vetch, or crimson clover.

How about watering?

Tomato and pepper roots will not grow without moisture. Regardless of where you live, the plants should be supplied with an inch of water every week. Whether you're in El Paso where natural rainfall is 7 inches annually, or in Tennessee where you get 60 to 70 inches of rain annually, it doesn't matter. If God doesn't give it to the plants, you will have to.

Water deeply to encourage maximum root development. In this area you should irrigate about once a week, depending on the temperature and wind. Remember that the larger your plants are, the more water they will need.

What about fertilizing?

I like to compare plants to people. If you fertilize sporadically, it's like feeding your family at Thanksgiving and not again until the next holiday. They wouldn't be very happy. Plants like to eat regularly. One of the most important things that you can do to get a bumper crop of tomatoes and peppers is use a starter solution when you put in your transplants. You can use a commercially available product or make your own by mixing 2 level tablespoons of super phosphate in 1 gallon of water. Pour about a cup of this in each transplant hole. Then, side-dress the plants with nitrogen every 2 to 3 weeks, beginning when the fruit is still tiny.

Slow-release fertilizers are great things. Not only does it avoid polluting water, but it provides nutrition over a long period of time.

What conditions will give you the best tomatoes?

The warmer it is, the firmer the fruit will be. The first tomatoes can be mushy, like those greenhouse-grown ones you buy in the grocery store. Also they must have plenty of sunlight. An abundance—or lack—of light will affect the flavor of the tomatoes.

One of the most common mistakes we see is that people try to grow crops in the shade. You have to have 8 to 10 hours of direct sunlight every day. I call it "sunbathing sun." Anything that

---

CONDITIONS FOR THE
BEST TOMATOES

- Plant as soon after last frost as possible for long growing season
- Warm temperatures for setting fruit—the hotter it is, the firmer the fruit
- Plenty of light
- Rich, well-drained soils
- Ample moisture
- Regular feeding
- Pick at height of maturity

sets fruit has to have sun. Ideally, you'll get full morning sun up until about 3 P.M. and then you'll have a little shade from the late afternoon sun.

What are some of the best tomato varieties to grow in this area?

Probably the very best is 'Merced'. You'll get your first crop of globe-shaped tomatoes about 75 to 80 days after putting in the transplants in spring. It's adaptable to a wide geographic range and has firm, bright red meat and a delicious flavor. Of course, we know that flavor is absolutely a personal thing. Whenever we have a blind taste test, everyone chooses a different favorite.

Other good varieties include 'Heatwave', which is a heat-setting, large-fruited variety; 'Surefire', which produces medium sized, tasty fruit; and 'Sunmaster', which has high yields of large fruit.

Do you grow both sweet and hot peppers here?

Yes. Like the taste test for the tomatoes, what some people consider hot, others consider mild. There are some folks with "Yankee lips" that can look at a hot pepper and get burnt and other folks who can eat peppers so hot we call them "hospital hot."

One of the best sweet bell peppers is 'Capistrano'. It's replacing the old standards because it produces bigger fruit and more of it. For something that ripens to yellow, we recommend 'Summer Sweet 860'.

For a hot pepper, we recommend 'Grande Hybrid Jalapeno', which is a hybrid with large fruit that matures from dark green to red.

Any other advice?

Be sure to keep the fruit picked to keep that plant producing, keep them watered and mulched—and enjoy. Harvest the fruit at the peak of maturity. And to determine the best size and color—observe what it looks like in the supermarket.

MARY NELL AND REX LEMERT
Amarillo: Home Gardeners

The yard in front of Mary Nell and Rex Lemert's beautiful home in Amarillo looks as traditional as any in the neighborhood, but walk around back and a delightful surprise awaits. The Lemerts' backyard has been transformed into a miniature farm, where every inch of space is used to produce a great bounty of fresh vegetables for this urban couple.

Although they did not start out as gardeners, their love of

digging in the soil and their appreciation for homegrown vegetables gradually changed them into happily passionate gardeners. Rex says that his mother gardened all the years he was growing up, and although he enjoyed the food, he did not choose to participate much in the garden. But when he and Mary Nell moved to Amarillo, he was spending long hours at the office and gardening became a good way to spend time outside. When they started a vegetable garden, Mary Nell said she couldn't believe they were going to "farm our backyard!" But she soon became so proficient at cooking tasty meals from the fresh produce that they quickly became spoiled by eating foods only a few minutes old.

When they added on to their house several years ago, they redesigned the entire garden to make it as low-maintenance as they could. They put in a sprinkler system and designed the beds so that they would have to do as little weeding as possible. Today, their small garden is overflowing with good things to eat and every inch of space is used to produce the vegetables, fruits, and herbs that they enjoy. They produce enough food to have fresh vegetables on the table from late April through September and have enough to share with friends and family. "Once you get used to eating homegrown vegetables," Mary Nell says, "nothing else tastes quite the same."

What is it like to garden in Amarillo, Texas?

It's certainly a challenge! Although we can have a light freeze as early as September, normally our first hard freeze is around October 13 or 14, and November can be really cold. In 1997, we had snow on April 15. And as it begins to get warm in May, we often have to contend with hailstorms, which can virtually destroy a garden in a matter of minutes.

How do you handle all that?

We grow many things from seed and just grow enough to replant if we need to. We try new

Hot pepper

STARTING FROM SEED

- Begin in February to plant in the garden in March or April.
- Sow seeds in a good seedling medium in 3-inch peat containers.
- Put trays 6–8 inches from grow lamps; as seeds sprout, move lights up.
- Water with a spray bottle set for light spray. After seedlings have emerged, pour water onto roots rather than spray foliage.
- After three weeks, begin fertilizing with weak liquid plant food.
- Harden off seedlings 2–3 days in shade outdoors before planting them in the garden.

---

things every year to see what's going to perform best for our area. We keep good records and record the temperature and rainfall and anything that might help us from year to year. The soil temperature is reported in the paper every Sunday and we pay attention to that when we begin to plant.

Is there any way to protect against hail?

Not really. You can use frost row cover, which helps some, but usually you just have to replant. We start enough seedlings to be able to replant several times if it's necessary.

We also have trouble with birds eating the seedlings, but you just learn to replant and not worry about it.

Do you start many plants indoors from seed or do you seed directly into the garden?

Almost everything is started indoors. We begin in February, so things are ready to put out by the end of March or early April. We start just about everything under grow lights. We sow the seeds in trays, which we put 6 to 8 inches from the grow lamps. As the seedlings sprout and grow, we move the lights up. After three weeks, we begin fertilizing with a liquid plant food.

What kind of containers do you use to start the seeds in?

We use primarily 3-inch peat containers. Even though I know you can put the peat containers right into the ground, we usually cut them away anyway. I'm not sure that they will decompose quickly enough to get the roots established well. We really like the peat containers, though, because they are inexpensive and come in all sizes.

The plants that we save indoors for planting later, I pot up into bigger containers.

What kind of soil mixture do you use for starting seeds?

The first thing I ever used was Jiffy Mix™ and I'm still using that today. We've always had good success with it, so why switch?

How do you actually plant the seeds?

I usually just follow the instructions on the seed package as to how deep to plant them, although almost everything is covered with $1/8$- to $1/4$-inch of soil mix. I then water the mixture carefully and cover the containers with a clear plastic covering which keeps the humidity right for the seeds to germinate. In this part of the country, where our humidity is low, it's essential for good seed germination.

How do you water the little seedlings?

While the seeds are still germinating, I use a spray bottle with the nozzle set for a light spray. Once they've emerged and I put them under the grow lamps, I remove the nozzle from the sprayer and pour the water into each container daily. I try hard not to spray or wet the leaves because I'm afraid of rot and mildew. I may act a little paranoid about this, but when I fertilize, I mix it in the bottle and pour it carefully. I don't risk wetting the leaves or burning them.

When do you thin the seedlings? When do you repot the seedlings, and when do you take them outdoors?

I begin thinning when the seedlings are 1 to 5 days old. This is also when I put them under the grow lights. The earlier the better, really. The plants that have been thinned and receive the most light are the strongest and the most vigorous plants. I don't repot them unless I don't have room in the garden for them at that time or if I want to grow them in containers for some reason. Fortunately, plants and seedlings want to survive. As gardeners, we simply have to provide the right environment for the seedling to do its natural thing. You really have to be negligent to fail.

It's hard to explain when to take the seedlings outdoors. More than anything else, you just look at the plant and decide. However, the optimum time seems to be when the seedlings are 5 to 7 inches tall and have good color.

How big is your garden? How is it constructed?

We have three beds that measure 4 × 12 feet and one that is 12 × 6 feet. They are all raised beds lined with plastic and filled with good topsoil. The sides of the beds are railroad ties. We found that the height of three ties was perfect for sitting down to weed. The plastic on the bottom has really helped keep down the weeds.

We add new soil and organic matter every year and the soil keeps getting better and better. We add peat moss and manure and hay to help build up the soil.

We've gardened in other places where we just took out the grass and began to plant, but it took a long time before it would produce well. The raised beds have done very well.

When do you actually start planting in the garden and what do you put into it?

We transplant in March when the soil temperature is at least 50°. We harden off the seedlings 2 to 3 days in the shade outdoors before I put them into the garden. I bring them out first thing in the morning, then bring them back inside the first night.

In late March to mid-April we begin planting the garden with four or five different kinds of lettuces, spinach, beets, and Swiss chard. Last year we planted some spinach varieties that did better than any we'd tried before. They were 'Italian Summer Savoy' and Dutch spinach 'Nordic IV'.

We like the Swiss chard better

than almost anything else. We probably eat it four times a week. We just put it in a frying pan with a little olive oil and fresh garlic, let it wilt, flip it once, and eat. It's wonderful. It's also very good for you. Chard is a tough plant that will tolerate a lot of cold weather.

What do you put into a summer garden?

All the usual hot weather crops—peppers, squash, eggplant, and tomatoes. We don't have enough room to do beans and we don't have a lot of sun, but it's amazing what we get out of such a small plot of land.

It's important to make sure the garden has a good rest in between planting seasons. During the cold months, I add manure and compost and turn it two or three times between October and March. This allows the organic matter to break down in the soil and help build it back up.

How do you make such a little space produce so much?

First, I make sure that the garden has a good rest in between planting seasons. I put it to bed in the middle of October, add manure and compost, and turn it two or three times between October and March. This allows the organic matter to break down in the soil and help build it back up.

During the growing season, though, I really push production. I begin as early as possible planting the cool-weather crops. The chard and arugula will last through the season, although we have to constantly cut back the arugula since it tends to bolt in the hot weather.

Then, I interplant things that mature at different times. For example, I plant beets and radishes in the same row. The beets take longer to mature than the radishes, so I thin the beet row when I harvest the radishes.

I have no patience with plants that don't produce, and grow plenty of extra seedlings with which to replace them. For example, if the spinach and lettuce are doing well, I leave them alone. If they are not producing that year, for whatever reason, then I will pull them out and replant them with sprouts of warm-weather crops. I may be early in putting in a lot of the hot-weather plants, but if they survive, they produce earlier and longer.

We never know from one year to the next what produce we will get from this garden, but we always have reserves waiting in the background to replace the crops which aren't performing. We always have production of some sort.

Do you fertilize?

Every couple of weeks, I'll get a bag of garden fertilizer and throw it out underneath the plants.

To get as much from the garden as possible, we plant cool-weather crops early and interplant things that mature at different times. If something does not produce well, I pull it out and replant it with something else.

Which herbs do you have good success with?

I love the basils and have had luck with anise basil, 'Siam Queen Thai', green broadleaf, and Thai lemon. Rosemary does fairly well, though not like it does in South or East Texas. Lemon thyme is easier to grow and is not nearly as delicate as French thyme. Sorrel does well and is easy to sprout, and dill does great and comes back year after year, although it does a rather nasty worm. We grow garlic because our ̱or's backyard is about one-third garlic and he shares with us, but it obviously does well here.

The kind of oregano that we get from the nurseries here grows really well, but we have to treat it as an ornamental since it has little flavor. Chives usually do well in our area, although I've had a difficult time growing them in my own garden for some reason.

Beelbalm goes wild and will even survive our winters with a little protection.

Resources

Sources of Seeds and Plants

Alliance Nursery
Route 1
Box 433
Marianna, FL 32446
Source for Southern fruit varieties

Berry Country Farms
P.O. Box 657
Brownsboro, TX 75756
903-882-3550
Berry specialists

Cottle Nursery
Route 1 Box 6
Fainson, NC 28341
919-267-4531
Strawberry plant nursery

Hudson (J.L.) Seedsman
P.O. Box 1058
Redwood City, CA 94064
Many heirloom and unusual vegetable varieties

Just Fruits
Route 2
Box 4818
Crawfordville, FL 32327
904-926-5644
Many unusual fruits good for the South

Papaya Tree Nursery
12422 El Oro Way
Granada Hills, CA 91344
818-363-3680
Tropical and semitropical plants

Plants of the Southwest
1812 Second Street
Santa Fe, NM 87501
Good for chiles and Southwestern plants

Rainbow Star Nursery
2324 Southwest 36th Terrace
Gainesville, FL 32607
904-378-4681

Redwood City Seed Co.
P.O. Box 361
Redwood City, CA 94064
Nice list of Asian vegetables

Shepherd's Garden Seeds
30 Irene Street
Torrington, CT 06790
Asian and European varieties

Tomato Grower's Supply
Company
P.O Box 2237
Fort Myers, FL 33902
Tomatoes and peppers

Wilhite Seed Company
P.O. Box 23
Poolville, TX 76487
French vegetables, melons

Display Gardens

Harris County Display Gardens
#2 Abercrombie Drive
Houston, TX 77084

Organizations

California Rare Fruit Growers,
Inc.
Fullerton Arboretum
California State University
Fullerton, CA 92634

North American Fruit Explorers
Rt. 1 Box 94
Chapin, IL 62628

Rare Fruit Council International
12255 Southwest 73rd Avenue
Miami, FL 33156

Southern Fruit Fellowship
c/o David E. Ulmer
P.O. Box 14606
Santa Rosa, CA 95402

Publications

BOOKS

Adams, William D. and Thomas
R. Leroy. *Commonsense
Vegetable Gardening for the
South.* Dallas, TX: Taylor
Publishing Company, 1995.

———. *Growing Fruits and Nuts
in the South.* Dallas, TX:
Taylor Publishing Company,
1992.

Brookbank, George. *Desert
Gardening.* Tuscon, AZ:
Fisher Books, 1991.

Bubel, Nancy. *Country Journal
Book of Vegetable Gardening.*
Harrisburg, PA: National
History Society, 1983.

Chambers, David and Lucinda
Mays. *Vegetable Gardening.*
New York: Knopf
Publishing/Pantheon Books,
1996.

Cotner, Sam. *The Vegetable Book:
A Texan's Guide to Gardening.*
Waco, TX: Gardener Press,
1986.

Cutler, Karen Davis. *The
Complete Vegetable and Herb
Gardener: A Guide to Growing
Your Garden Organically.*
Burpee Seeds, 1998.

Groom, Dale. *Texas Gardener's Guide: The What, Where, When, How and Why of Gardening in Texas.* Franklin, TN: Cool Springs Press, 1997.

Hastings, Don. *Gardening in the South with Don Hastings: Vegetables and Fruits.* Dallas, TX: Taylor Publishing Company, 1988.

Kramer, Jack. *Earthly Delights: Tubs of Tomatoes, Buckets of Beans.* Golden, CO: Fulcrum Publishing, 1997.

Luebberman, Mimi. *Heirloom Gardens: Simple Secrets for Old-Fashioned Flowers and Vegetables.* San Francisco, CA: Chronicle Books, 1997.

McEachern, George Ray. *Growing Fruits, Berries, and Nuts in the South.* Houston, TX: Gulf Coast Publishing Co., 1978.

Ortho. *All About Citrus and Subtropical Fruits.* San Ramon, CA: Ortho, 1985.

Sperry, Neil. *Neil Sperry's Complete Guide to Texas Gardening.* Dallas, TX: Taylor Publishing Company, 1991.

Walheim, Lance. *Citrus: Complete Guide to Selecting and Growing More Than 100 Varieties for California, Arizona, Texas, the Gulf Coast and Florida.* Tucson, AZ: Ironwood Press, 1996.

Watson, Benjamin (ed.). *Taylor's Guide to Heirloom Vegetables.* New York: Houghton Mifflin, 1996.

Weaver, William Woys and Peter Hatch. *Heirloom Vegetable Gardening: A Master Gardener's Guide to Planting, Growing, Seed Saving and Cultural History.* New York: Henry Holt and Co., 1997.

Internet

Julian Sauls has an excellent article on home citrus fruit production on the Web at <aggie-horticulture.tamu.edu>.

TREES AND SHRUBS

DAVID CREECH
Nacogdoches: Stephen F. Austin University

Professor of horticulture at Stephen F. Austin University, David Creech is a man with the rare ability to change his path to stay in step with his times. His background, which includes a bachelor's degree and doctorate in horticulture from Texas A&M University, had primarily been in pomology, with a particular interest in pecans, peaches, blueberries, and alternative fruits. One example of David's contributions to this field was the planting of the first blueberries in Texas, in 1965. Another was Creech's Peaches, a 3,500-tree peach orchard that he developed in the mid to late seventies. His passions also included such unusual crops as pawpaw, mayhaws, goomby berries, raisin tree, sausage vine, and jujubes—crops unusual in a Texas market.

"But in 1985, I woke up with very few students. The interest in traditional horticultural crops of fruits and vegetables had dwindled to almost nothing. The national trend had turned toward ornamentals. So I turned, too," David says. "It quickly became apparent that we needed a place for some hands-on experience, and the Arboretum came into being.

"We've been really fortunate. We were able to use the land along the LaNana Creek, and have had the support of both the community and the University. We struggled the first five to ten years, but lack of funding and lack of labor are always major hurdles. But we also had to deal with uncooperative weather.

"We now have ten acres and have planted around 3,000 plants. We hope it will become an evaluation center for new plants and a recipient of plant collections for the nursery industry. The mission of the Arboretum is simple: (1) to evaluate new landscape plant materials for the twenty-first century and (2) to promote the conservation, selection and use of the native plants of the South."

David Creech's turning point has resulted in a tremendous boon for East Texas. His boundless energy and considerable expertise has resulted in the Stephen F. Austin University Arboretum, a great resource both for home gardeners and professional growers.

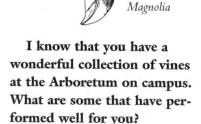

Magnolia

I know that you have a wonderful collection of vines at the Arboretum on campus. What are some that have performed well for you?

We have more wisterias and honeysuckles under test than anywhere else in the South, at least growing side by side for comparison. You have to be brave to plant vines, though. Many of them are rambunctious

growers and some don't behave all that well.

At the Arboretum we finally put the vines in a $3/4$-acre area near the LaNana Creek. Even though it floods occasionally, it gets full sun and the soil drains well.

We grow many different kinds of wisteria, including *W. sinensis, W. floribunda,* and *W. frutescens,* which is native to southeast Texas and is not as aggressive as the Asian species. It has a smaller leaf and bloom, but has both a blue and a white flowering form.

We have also tried the native honeysuckle, *Lonicera sempervirens,* and have about a dozen cultivars of this. We also love *Lonicera* × *americana.*

One of the showiest vines is the red-flowering cross vine, *Bignonia capreolata* 'Atrosanguinea'. Grown in full sun, this will put on an outstanding floral display.

Another great vine for a sunny spot is the Chinese trumpet creeper, *Campsis grandiflora* 'Morning Calm'. It has big, pink to salmon flowers that look almost like petunias.

What are some of the other collections that you have in the Arboretum?

We are proud of several collections. We have an extensive

WOODY PLANTS WITH PROMISE
Large Trees

Sweetgum	*Liquidambar styraciflua* 'Rotundiloba'
Dawn redwood	*Metasequoia glyptostroboides*
Mexican oaks	*Quercus polymorpha, Q. canbyi, Q. risophylla*
Wingnut	*Pterocarya stenoptera*
Montezuma cypress	*Taxodium mucronatum*
Japanese zelkova	*Zelkova serrata*

Magnolia planting and are now on a mission to plant sixty-five magnolia cultivars, including those with variegated foliage, yellow blossoms, and various foliage and tree forms that make up *Magnolia grandiflora* diversity in the South.

We have a growing collection of hollies that indicate many fine performers. Our Japanese holly (*Ilex crenata*) collection now contains over twenty-five cultivars. One of these, 'Sky Pencil', is one of the hot new plants for the South.

Another holly of great promise (it also serves as the logo for the Arboretum) is the American holly (*Ilex opaca*). It is such a common plant in the South that it is often taken for granted. It's slow to establish, but after the first few years, it has few problems with insects, disease, flooding, or drought. It's a plant for all seasons, with colorful berries, interesting bark, and good foliage. We are evaluating thirty different varieties of the common American holly, including those with yellow berries, different leaf shape, and dwarf growth form.

We also have quite a few crape myrtles. There are hundreds of varieties available, from ground covers to large trees.

The dry garden, soon to be named the Lynn Lowrey Memorial Dry Garden, is an exciting mix of western dry-loving, sun-loving species that show great promise as low maintenance landscape plants in East Texas. We are excited about this new garden.

The hosta and fern collection in the shade garden is also outstanding and worth a visit.

What are some of the things that you evaluate in these plants?

The same things that we

evaluate in fruits and vegetables: their adaptability to our area, how fast they grow, their resistance to disease and insects. It just takes a long time with the woody plants. We have to leave them in the ground for a long time, and we now have things in the Arboretum that we suspect are not going to be really good for the garden. But that's part of the evaluation process as well, to determine what's garden worthy. I want to include a wide variety of plant materials so that students, the public, and people from the nursery industry learn about plants.

What are some unusual or little-known plants good for East Texas gardens?

There are so many exciting new plants that it's hard to come up with a small list, but there are some that seem particularly outstanding. I think sweetspire (*Itea virginica*) is underutilized and should be seen more in the landscape.

Viburnum propinquum is a durable little evergreen glossy-leaved viburnum that breaks out a carpet of white flowers in late spring and is easy to manage at 3 to 4 feet—an unusual size for viburnum. Actually, there are many viburnums that deserve a place in East Texas landscapes.

Many *Styrax* family members

and varieties show good adaptation in our garden; the snowbells are special small trees that deserve greater recognition in our area.

One of my favorite rarely-seen plants is *Heptacodium miconioides*, the seven sons flower, which blooms in August with a wonderful cascade of white flowers that turn into attractive pink seed inflorescences.

Are there large trees that you have tested that look as if they will be good to include in the landscape?

One of the best seems to be the Montezuma cypress (*Taxodium mucronatum*). It looks as if it will be very hardy, having survived the '89 freeze as well as the '95 drought, although it did lose leaves in the drought. It seems worthy of planting in Houston and south. It has fewer problems with "knees" than many other cypress species.

We're also excited about the Mexican oaks, *Quercus polymorpha, Q. canbyi,* and *Q. risophylla*. These have tested out well in East Texas. They establish easily and fit into the landscape well. *Q. risophylla* is an evergreen, fast-growing oak with sandpaper texture on the dark green leaves. It has columnar

WOODY PLANTS WITH PROMISE

Small Trees and Large Shrubs

Japanese maples	*Acer palmatum* cultivars
Camphor tree	*Camphora officinalis*
Showy desert willow	*Chilopsis linearis* 'Bubba'
Blueberry hawthorn	*Crataegus brachyacantha*
Texas persimmon	*Diospyros texana*
Aralia	*Eleutherococcus sieboldianus* 'Variegatus'
Euschapis	*Euschapis japonica*
Juniper	*Juniperus virginiana* 'Grey Owl'
Mahonia	*Mahonia gracilis*
Texas pistache	*Pistacia texana*
Sinojackia	*Sinojackia rehderiana*
Texas mountain laurel	*Sophora secundiflora*
Styrax	*Styrax japonica*
Lacebark elm	*Ulmus parvifolia*
Viburnum	*Viburnum propinquum*

growth habit when young, which changes to a more open branching pattern as the tree matures.

The sweetgum cultivar, *Liquidambar styraciflua* 'Rotundiloba', shows great promise. It has rounded, lobed leaves and no fruit and is slow growing.

For a fast-growing tree, we recommend the wingnuts from China and Japan, *Pterocarya stenoptera* and *P. rhoifolia*. In the Arboretum, one grew so fast in six years that it shaded out many other plants. The seeds hang in long chains and are quite attractive.

How about smaller trees or shrubs?

We've gone nuts with the Japanese maples, *Acer palmatum*. We now have over 100 varieties growing in the Arboretum. There are many different forms and there seems to be something for everyone. Young trees, in particular, are prone to a leaf burn in late summer but this depends on their exposure to sun and wind. Eastern exposures have proven to be best for these small trees. The Japanese maples vary in height. *Acer ginnala*, the Amur maple, has found the Arboretum a good home and is now over 20 feet tall after ten years. The species sports outstanding red fall color when grown in full to partial sun.

The camphor tree (*Camphora officinalis*) looks like it will be a great garden addition for Southerners looking for an attractive broad-leaved evergreen. It seems to be very hardy, having survived temperatures below 11°.

Machilus thunbergii, native to Asia, is another broadleafed evergreen showing promise. It is a member of the *Magnolia* family and seems to be hardy, as long as the selections come from cold-hardy sites. Specimens of this growing in Aiken, South Carolina, have endured below-zero temperatures.

The blueberry hawthorn (*Crataegus brachyacantha*) is a small, showy tree good for informal or formal landscapes. The leaves are finely cut and it bears white flowers in spring.

For something with interesting bark, try the Texas persimmon (*Diospyros texana*). It has exfoliating white-gray bark and a unique branching structure. Another "must have" is the Texas mountain laurel (*Sophora secundiflora*). We feel that it's a great landscape plant that should be used more in East Texas. It has wonderful purple flowers that emit a sweet fragrance that is particularly strong in the early morning.

Mahonia (*Mahonia gracilis*) is a native of Mexico that has proven to be sturdy and hardy. There are several exciting *Mahonia* hybrids that are now named cultivars, and all are worthy of garden use and additional evaluation.

*T*o plant a tree or shrub, plant in fall, dig a wide hole only as deep as the root ball, and do not amend the soil. Add pine bark mulch 2 to 4 inches deep in a circle around the plant and water as frequently as needed.

What are some basic gardening tips for growing woody plants?

Key, to me, is what you do during the first couple of years to help get the plant well established. We usually plant in fall and begin by digging a wide hole that is only as deep as the root ball, whether this is a container-grown or ball-and-burlap plant. We do not amend the hole, believing in good soil-to-root contact at planting time.

After covering the root ball back up with soil, we put on pine bark mulch 2 to 4 inches deep in a circle around the plant and water as frequently as needed. Ample water is important, particularly during the first and second summers. We keep a weed-free circle around the plant and put on a light application of general purpose granular fertilizer every month or two during the growing season.

Mixed borders, whether herbaceous, woody, or both, provide the most fun and education and are often the most forgiving in terms of covering up plants that might not perform well.

Do you have any tips for including woody plants in a landscape design?

I maintain that a good design should include a backbone of proven performers. That is, at least 75 percent to 90 percent of the trees and shrubs in a landscape should be plants that have shown the ability to tolerate the conditions that we have—including a hard freeze and occasional dry and wet spells—and should

not need any special care or attention.

For the rest, however, the list of potential landscape standouts is immense. When you choose more adventuresome plants, be aware of the potential plant size at maturity, and the greatest seasons of interest. Be aware of combining color, texture, and form, and group them based on their sun, soil drainage, and moisture needs.

Mixed borders, whether herbaceous, woody, or both, provide the most fun and education and are often the most forgiving in terms of covering up plants that might not perform well.

When we designed the Arboretum, we did so based on a collection of small theme gardens. Not only is this aesthetically pleasing, this also allowed students to be involved with a specific garden area during their career. Students have said that they remember minute details about these gardens for years after they graduate and that it almost always brings up a good feeling.

What are some of the trees and shrubs that give good fall color in East Texas?

Red maple, Japanese maple, Amur maple, Florida maple, and many other *Acer* species are standouts. *Fothergilla gardenii* is an up-and-coming landscape plant in our area and fall color for this has been striking. The sweetspire can put on a show if it receives enough sun. The native rusty blackhaw viburnum (*Viburnum rufidulum*) can be a traffic stopper. It's hard to beat the Chinese pistache for vivid oranges and reds.

If I want a quick-growing woody plant to use as a screen, what would you suggest?

The leyland cypress, despite disease and insect problems, comes to mind. It's fast growing and drought tolerant, but shows little talent for growing old gracefully. Some of the new *Thuja plicata* and *T. orientalis* cultivars show promise, with fewer disease and insect problems.

Prunus caroliniana 'Compacta' looks sharp in the Arboretum. Some of the new *Cleyera* cultivars are excellent screening materials. *Myrica cerifera* makes an effective screen in just a few years, if cared for properly. There are many hollies that deserve use as a screening material. 'Nellie R. Stevens' is commonly used this way.

GLYN WHIDDON
Harlingen: Stuart Place Nursery

Originally from East Texas, Glyn Whiddon came to the Rio Grande Valley after getting his degree in landscape architecture from Texas A&M. Although he originally worked with a garden center and landscape company, he soon went into business for himself and established his own design/build landscape firm in 1976.

When the hard freezes of '89 and '93 came around, plant material was scarce and what he could find had, for the most part, been brought in from California to be sold at inflated prices. This combination inspired Glyn to begin to grow some of the plants for the business himself. He was so successful at it and had so much plant material on hand that he soon opened the

Hibiscus

retail store, Stuart Place Nursery, which was soon followed by Rain Forest Wholesale Nursery.

What is the growing climate like in your region?

In the lower Rio Grande Valley, which is basically south of Corpus Christi and east of Loredo and includes Brownsville, Harlingen, and McAllen, we are a subtropical region. We are the same latitude as Miami but we receive half the annual rainfall. This means that we have to be very selective in the type of plant material we choose because of our soil types and lack of precipitation. In general, we have alkaline, clay soils with a lot of salt. Our water supply is from the Rio Grande River, which is also salty.

What are some of the basic landscape plants for your area?

Palms—of which there are many varieties—hibiscus, bougainvillea, and oleander are the most common. Other tropical plants include bird of paradise, *Philodendron*, cycads, and croton.

Are all these reliably hardy here?

In most years. Last year we had only one frost. That was not typical—El Niño was kind to us. We usually have a few light freezes but usually no hard freezes. That allows us to use a wide range of tropical materials. Strong and frequent Gulf winds are also a factor.

It is generally the lack of water, rather than the cold, that is the limiting factor. Right now we are suffering from a severe water shortage. Everyone is careful with what they plant. For a long time now I've promoted the use of xeriscape-type plant material here. We have a nice mixture of plants that is tropical looking, yet has low water requirements.

What are some of the other tropical plants that you use in the landscape?

Everyone wants to use citrus. This is the home of the Rio Red grapefruit. Other popular plants include limes, lemons, oranges, bananas, papayas, agave, and Hollywood juniper.

Which palms work well for the area?

There are quite a few, although those that are hardy and perform the best are not necessarily those that are the most popular. Some of the hardier varieties should be used more often, things such as the Chinese fan palm, the Mediterranean fan palm, and the King sago, which is a little slower growing than the species

Washingtonia robusta, more commonly used because it grows faster.

Do most gardeners here want to plant a tropical-looking landscape and take advantage of the trees that you can grow here?

Almost everyone does. There are a few translocated "snowbirds" that don't like the look. They want their lilacs and hostas, but they learn to adapt to the climate and plant what will grow. We recommend that people plant a combination of native and adapted plants. One of the prettiest flowering trees here is the native wild olive (*Cordia boissieri*), a small tree, similar to the crape myrtle in size with rough bark and a rough-textured leaf. It produces big clusters of single white flowers shaped like a petunia and blooms constantly during the warm months of the year.

Other non-native flowering trees that do well for us include the crape myrtle, particularly the mildew-resistant varieties such as 'Baskam's Party Pink' and 'Nachez'. We also use the orchid tree (*Bauhinia purpurea*), which attracts hummingbirds; and royal poinciana, kapok, jacaranda, tabebuia, and golden shower tree.

Which of the hibiscus varieties do you like?

Hibiscus is a great plant here and there are many collectors. We even use it as hedge material. People like to grow both the old standbys and the new varieties as well. Those with the single blooms are probably the hardiest—varieties such as 'Indian Chief'. But many people grow the exotic varieties too, even though they don't bloom as well and they are not as hardy. I like 'Hula Girl', which produces a bright yellow single flower with a red throat.

Are there display gardens in the area that show many of the hibiscus cultivars?

At Stuart Place Nursery, we have some plantings where we test new varieties of ornamentals and herbs for their adaptability to our region. I go to California and Florida often to find out what other people are working with and often bring back new varieties to try here.

Have you introduced plants that were new to this region?

Many years ago, I began working with buttercup, *Turnera*, which is a great plant. It is a low-growing tropical shrub that grows to 3 feet and produces a single yellow petunia-sized bloom. I also helped popularize some of the flowering vines such as the Maylay rubber vine (*Cryptostegia grandiflora*).

Are there other seldom-used landscape plants that you feel have great potential for gardens in your area?

I really like bulbine (*Bulbine caulescens*), which is fleshy and similar to aloe vera. It is native to South Africa, puts forth a spike of orange flowers, and has a long season of bloom.

We encourage people to plant according to the amount of time and effort they want to spend in the garden. If you love to spend time in your garden, then plant to your heart's content.

For someone just beginning to garden in your area, how do you suggest that they select plant material for their gardens?

Observe what is growing in other gardens close by. Talk to professionals and ask for their recommendations.

What is the biggest gardening challenge here?

The soil. Through the valley we have bands of different soil types so that we range from sand to heavy clay. Having a soil test done at a County Extension Office is important. Usually the recommendation is to work with the native soil and to add organic matter whenever possible. Amendments such as peat moss, ground pine bark, and good compost are always good to put into the soil.

Are there pests and diseases that you battle?

The sweet potato whitefly is probably the worst. It began in Florida and migrated here. It is a tiny whitefly that eats just about everything, and all stages of it are damaging. It sucks the chlorophyll out of the leaf and ruins all kinds of plants—food crops as well as ornamentals—particularly anything related to the cotton family. Really the only thing a home owner can do is to spray with a tiny amount of liquid soap in water and be persistent. You can't use too much of the soapy water at any one time or it will burn the leaves.

We also have problems with fungus due to our high humidity. Even though our rainfall is low, our humidity is high because we're close to the coast. To prevent mildew and fungus, we recommend good air circulation between the plants.

What are the different growing seasons here?

Fall is the main planting season for bedding plants. This is when we put in plants such as petunias, impatiens, calendula, and gerber daisies. When you plant these in fall, they will last through spring until hot weather hits. When planting in fall, however, be sure to wait until the really hot weather has passed. Generally around September 1, we begin planting cool weather crops such as lettuce, spinach, carrots, broccoli, cauliflower, and brussels sprouts. In summer, it's too hot for many vegetables, although we do grow some tomatoes. Peppers are a godsend for us and we grow every kind of pepper imaginable. Summer bedding plants include periwinkle, purslane, moss rose, marigolds, and zinnias.

Do you have any other advice?

We encourage people to plant according to the amount of time they want to spend in the garden. If you're a true gardener and love to spend time in your garden, then plant to your heart's content. But if you're not going to take care of it, don't plant that way.

GLYN WHIDDON FAVORITES

Bulbine	*Bulbine caulescens*
Golden shower tree	*Cassia fistula*
Wild olive	*Cordia boissieri*
Maylay rubber vine	*Cryptostegia grandiflora*
Royal poinciana	*Delonix regia*
Hibiscus	*Hibiscus* sp.
Jacaranda	*Jacaranda mimosifolia*

LINDA GAY
Houston: Mercer Arboretum

PLANTS FOR FALL

Petunias
Impatiens
Calendula
Gerber daisy
Lettuce
Spinach
Carrots
Broccoli
Cauliflower
Brussels sprouts

Linda Gay is a woman who loves to learn. From horticulture school at Trident Technical College in Charleston, South Carolina, to her present position as acting director of Mercer Arboretum near Houston, she makes a point to learn something every day. "I worked for a landscape company for a while, but after I learned about the green industry, my job consisted of mowing and spraying and sticking to a schedule and there wasn't much opportunity to keep learning about plants. It just wasn't for me."

In 1985 she came to Mercer Arboretum and has been instrumental in developing it into the outstanding public garden that it is today. Within the 262 acres encompassed by the Arboretum, Linda has continued to learn and expand her knowledge of plants and gardening—and to share this knowledge with the visitors who come to stroll the red brick paths or to examine in close detail the outstanding collections that make up part of the garden. She has been instrumental in developing an outstanding collection of tropical plants—a challenge in Houston, Texas.

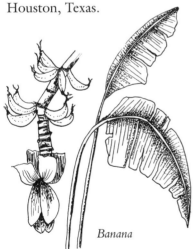

Banana

What are some of the advantages to growing tropical plants?

Tropical plants offer a great diversity of colors and textures, and have wonderfully fragrant, exotic flowers. In the Houston area, they perform well for nine months (or more, when we have mild winters) and are happiest in the hottest, most humid growing season we know! By living on the Gulf Coast, we have an advantage. We can use material that overlaps from two distinctly different growing regions. Some plants from the Northeast acclimate, and some from Florida freeze to the ground but return from the roots the following year.

Can you grow tropical plants in Houston?

We can easily grow the plants that have a tropical appearance and are hardy to our area. The true tropicals, which die when temperatures dip below 32°, are a little more difficult. Some of these can be used in the garden in containers and pulled back indoors when frost comes; others can be planted in the ground, allowed to die back to the roots in the winter and return in the spring.

The majority of plants we have on display in the tropical section are dug up and brought into the greenhouses to overwinter. We have two 30 × 90-foot greenhouses for this purpose. But, since we have nine months of growing season here, it just doesn't make sense not to take advantage of some of these fabulous plants.

Tropical plants offer a great diversity of colors and textures. They have wonderfully fragrant, exotic flowers, and in the Houston area, they perform well for nine months, or longer if we have a mild winter.

Are tropicals a new and coming thing in the Houston gardening world?

I think many people have grown them as patio, courtyard, or atrium plants, but with our ever-changing winters, people are planting them into the garden for their ease of maintenance and to enjoy a more mature plant.

Also, many new tropical plants that are coming in from Florida add to the choices we have. At Mercer, we have tropical tours and plant sales every summer and both are well attended, which tells me that tropicals are gaining in popularity.

If you don't have a greenhouse where you can overwinter these plants, how do you grow tropicals?

You can treat them as annuals, taking cuttings to propagate so you don't have to start all over again every year. Or, you can just dig them up and put them into the garage for the winter. For example, many people do this with plumeria because that is a plant that will need protection. Water it about once a month or put it into a container so that it won't dry out so quickly. Sometimes we leave plants in containers all year long and just plant the whole thing outdoors in summer and lift it in the fall.

Devoted tropical-plant people will plant close to the house or in a small area so that they can actually put up a little plastic-covered quonset hut over the plants when cold weather comes. It's like setting up a small, temporary greenhouse. We only have cold weather usually for three or four nights. Frost row cover also helps.

Finding a microclimate in your own yard is probably the best thing to do. Many of our gardens are quite shady because they're found under pine or oak trees. If you plant in a spot such as that, the trees help protect the plants from frost and offer some protection from the north wind. Also, you can plant on the south side of the house or next to a wall that gives some protection.

TIPS FOR GROWING
TROPICALS (NORTH OF
THE TROPICS)

- Find a microclimate in your own yard.
- Plant under trees or next to a wall that will offer some protection.
- Plant on the south side of the house.
- If possible, wrap the plant with frost cloth to protect against cold temperatures.

You also learn to work with the plants to help them survive the cold. For example, when a hard freeze has been predicted, we go out and cut the fronds off the Australian tree fern that we grow here. Then we cover the plant with frost cloth, wrap it with plastic, and leave it like that for 2 or 3 months. The plant never misses a beat. It's protected in a shady spot and when we uncover it in early spring, it's just fine. But putting it in the right spot to begin with helps tremendously.

What are some of the plants that you can use in a shady garden?

Bromeliads, rhizomatous and cane begonias, gingers, coleus, caladiums, tropical palms, and *Strobilanthes*, commonly known as Persian shield.

What could you use in a sunny spot?

Bananas are great. Many people will allow the trees to die down to the ground during winter, but if you ever want it to bear fruit, you have to protect the trunks from winter cold. We teach gardeners to wrap the trunk with an old blanket or frost cloth and cover the whole plant with plastic. The trees have to be at least two years old before they start bearing fruit anyway. In late February or March you can see green pushing through and when you first uncover it, you might lose a few of the first leaves, but then it leafs out and flowers. Because it takes so long for the fruit to ripen, when you see small bunches of bananas, go ahead and cut the flower off to hasten the ripening process.

Some people grow just the ornamental bananas because the regular banana takes up too much room in a home garden. There are many, many different kinds such as *Musa ornata*, which has an upright flower. It gets to be about 10 feet tall and has a lavender vein underneath the leaf and a lavender flower. *Musa velutina* is smaller, only growing about 6 feet tall.

The angel trumpets, *Brugmansia*, are beautiful for a

sunny spot. They are fast growing and will reach a height of 8 to 10 feet during a single growing season. When it freezes, they'll die back to the roots but will come up again the next year. They have light green leaves with stunning white, pink, or yellow flowers that are fragrant in the early morning and late evening.

What is the difference between angel trumpet and daturas?

They were all in the *Datura* genus, but because angel trumpet flowers are pendulous, they were separated into the class *Brugmansias*. *Datura* flowers are held erect or facing outward and seed readily; *Brugmansias* are reliably root hardy and reach 12 to 15 feet. *Daturas'* maximum height is about 5 feet.

What are other tropical favorites?

Alocasia sp., elephant ear or taro plant, is root hardy so you can leave it in the ground. You can also use this in a water garden. *A. plumbea,* the purple variety, is marginal as a bog plant. This plant likes some shade. If it gets too much sun, you might have trouble with spider mites. It's a great texture to work with, and both texture and color are important considerations when you design a garden.

Gingers are becoming enormously popular. Are these hardy in your area?

Quite a few are hardy up to horticultural Zone 8b. They can be divided into different groups: the *Hedychiums*, or butterfly gingers; the *Costus*, or spiral gingers; the *Curcumas*, or hidden gingers; the *Kaempferia*, peacock or groundcover gingers; and *Zingiber*, the common edible gingers.

People should start with the easy-to-grow butterfly gingers. They are called this because the individual flowers look like butterflies. They are highly fragrant and grow 6 to 8 feet tall and can take more sun than the other gingers. If you have been growing these and they don't bloom well or they grow horizontally instead of upright, they probably need more sun. They will tolerate heavy, wet soils—and might even grow in the water. *Hedychium gardnerianum* 'Kahili' takes over in Hawaii. It has a yellow bloom with red stamen. Once it's established, the leaves can get 4 inches across. It's good as a background plant or for cut flowers.

A species that colonizes well is *H. aurantiacum*. The fragrance is not strong or overpowering, but if you bring it indoors, it will add a nice, subtle fragrance to the room.

The *Hedychiums* have an interesting growth form. After the second year, they move around. They put out rhizomes on top of the ground. To get a clump full in the center again, cut these rhizomes every 4 to 6 inches and leave three or four nodes between cuts.

What do the *Curcumas* look like?

They're generally very exotic looking. You see them often in the cut flower trade. They are called "hidden gingers" because the foliage comes up and often hides the flowers. The spring bloomers, however, put up the flowering stem and bloom before the foliage appears. These must have afternoon shade. These are great to have in the garden because they bloom in late February and early March and help usher in the spring. They appear so early, though, that sometimes they get caught by a late cold snap, and if the temperatures drop into the forties, they are very unhappy. If they get cold, the leaves turn bright yellow overnight. They like rich, light soil. The beds should be reworked every five years or so to keep the soil from becoming compacted.

The *Kaempferias*, or peacock gingers, love the shade and are very happy if they get no direct sunlight. The foliage is wonderful and shows different patterns. Too much sun, though, causes the leaves to roll up. *Kaempferia rotunda* has a tall (18- to 20-inch), erect leaf with purple and white orchid-like flowers. It produces beautiful clusters of fragrant flowers that grow close to the ground. The flowers are about the size of a half dollar and have no stem. They don't make a good cut flower, but they look very exotic in the landscape. *K. roscoeana* has leaves that are 12 inches wide and are wonderfully patterned.

Most *Kaempferias* grow 4 inches tall or less. They make a wonderful ground cover and are sometimes called the "southern hosta."

This group is the last to come up in spring and the last to go down in fall. But from April until frost, the foliage makes a wonderful accent plant in the garden.

How do you care for the gingers throughout the year?

Regular watering and good drainage are both important. Ideally, you should plant them in spring. Fall planting is usually a gamble. Because we don't really

PLANTS FOR TROPICAL GARDENING ON THE GULF COAST

Those marked **T** are tender, meaning that they have to be protected from the cold or treated as an annual. **RH** means root hardy. These will die back to the ground but reappear the following year. **H** indicates a hardy or frost-resistant plant. **A** indicates an annual, many of which reseed themselves.

Chenille plant (Evergreen)	*Acalypha hispida*	H
Taro	*Alocasia* sp.	RH
Tailflower	*Anthurium podophyllum*	T
Hop-headed barleria	*Barleria lupulina*	RH
Dwarf tree fern	*Blechnum gibbum*	T
Pink snowbush	*Breynia disticha* 'Roseo-Picta'	T
Angel trumpet	*Brugmansia* hybrid	RH
Canna	*Canna* hybrid 'Durban'	RH
Calathea	*Calathea* 'Green Ice'	T
Brazilian button flower	*Centratherum* sp.	A
Java glorybower	*Clerodendrum speciosissimum*	RH
Kaffir lily	*Clivia* sp.	T
Croton	*Codiaeum* hybrid	T
Crinum	*Crinum asiaticum*	RH
Horn-of-plenty	*Datura metel*	A
Flax lily (Evergreen)	*Dianella* sp.	RH
Yerba mala	*Euphorbia cotinifolia*	T
Blue daze	*Evolvulus pilosis* 'Blue Daze'	T
Mexican hamelia	*Hamelia erecta*	RH
Parrot flower	*Heliconia psittacorum*	T
Lobster claw	*Heliconia rostrata*	T
Waffle plant	*Hemigraphis alternata*	T

Morning glory tree	*Ipomea fistulosa*	RH
Jungle geranium	*Ixora coccinea*	T
Coral plant	*Jatropha multifida*	T
White shrimp plant	*Justicia brandegeana*	RH
Lion's ear	*Leonotis leonurus*	RH
Tapioca	*Manihot esculenta*	T
Bananas	*Musa* sp.	RH
Poinsettia tree	*Mussaenda luteola*	T
Firefern	*Oxalis hedysaroides* 'Rubra'	T
Frangipani	*Plumeria* hybrid	T
Chocolate plant	*Pseuderanthemum elatum*	RH
Tropical sage	*Salvia miniata*	A
Fan flower	*Scaevola aemula* 'Blue Wonder'	A
Skullcap	*Scutellaria* 'Purple Fountains'	A
Cat's whiskers	*Tacca chantrieri*	A
Princess flower	*Tibouchina urvilleana*	RH
Yellow alder	*Turnera ulmifolia*	T
Malanga	*Xanthosoma*	T

have a fall season, there's little time for plants to root in. It goes from hot summer to cold winter quickly. You have to get these established before a hard frost comes or they will not survive.

You should feed them in spring with a high nitrogen fertilizer, but be careful not to add phosphorous because our soils are naturally high in phosphorous anyway. A topdressing of compost in summer gives them a nice boost.

Where should you include gingers in the landscape?

They look beautiful interplanted among native trees, but you have to be careful to keep them watered. The trees will take water from the smaller, herbaceous plants so be sure to give them supplemental watering during dry periods.

MORRIS CLINT
*Brownsville: Palm Gardens
Nursery*

Morris Clint, owner of Palm
Gardens Nursery in Brownsville,
gives his parents credit for his
lifelong passion for plants. "We
were a close family with lots of
love going around. My father
was very clever, too. One year
when I was just a little kid running around in short pants,
maybe nine or ten years old, the
garden was attacked by grass-
hoppers and my Dad offered
me a bounty of half-a-cent per
grasshopper. Not only did I
amass a small fortune for a little
guy, I also began a lifetime interest in plants and nature. From
then on, I've been a gardener at
heart."

Morris's parents were unusually knowledgeable and interested
in plants and often spent week-
ends and vacations traveling
through Mexico looking for
orchids, bromeliads, ferns, cacti,
and bulbs. His mother made a
name for herself growing and
breeding *Amaryllis* and collecting *Zephyranthes*.

When Morris left home to
attend Texas A&M College,
as it was called at that time, he
studied floriculture. After gradu-
ation, he went to Auburn
University to manage the orna-

mental horticulture greenhouses
there. When he returned to
Brownsville in 1953, he started
his own nursery business.

Plumeria

**Do you specialize in any
one kind of plant at the
nursery?**

I really try to encourage people to use palms in the landscape.
When we first started this business, we had planted seventy-
eight different kinds of palms on
the property, but we got our ears
knocked down in '82 when we
had a bad freeze. Only thirteen
varieties survived that freeze. I
kept those that survived and
built our present collection
around those survivors.

**What are some of the hardy
palms that you can grow here?**

One of the hardiest and the
most common is the Chinese fan
palm (*Livistona chinensis*), which
grows slowly to 20 to 30 feet

tall. Others include the European fan palm (*Chamaerops humilis*), and gru gru (*Acrocomia totai*), which has thorns all up and down the trunk and on the leaves. This is well adapted but extremely scarce. *Sabal texana* has gained popularity after surviving a major freeze. It is very tough but slow growing.

There are others that are hardy but which we've had insect and virus problems with, such as almost the entire genus of *Phoenix* palms, including the Canary Island date palm. Only a few pockets of this tree are left, although it used to be quite prevalent. A disease similar to the lethal yellow virus found in Florida wiped out almost all of them.

We also used to grow quite a

few Queen palms (*Arecastrum*, formerly *Cocos plumosa*), but we've had problems with it, too. The most commonly used palm is *Washingtonia robusta*. Also seen is *Phoenix roebelenii*, a dwarf to 7 to 10 feet that is not affected by lethal yellows but is subject to hard freezes. Jelly palm, *Cocos australis* (now *Butia capitata*), is very hardy.

Are there other plants that you use in the landscape?

I'm very fond of cycads. The most rugged is probably *Cycas revoluta*, the common sago palm. Another good one is the queen sago (*Cycas circinalis*). I also like the cardboard palm (*Zamia furfuracea*); a clumping palm from the Yucatan peninsula (*Paurotis wrightii*); and the low-growing coontie palm (*Zamia pumila*).

How about flowering ornamental trees?

There are many that we use here and that add so much to our landscapes. The most eye-catching is the sunshine tree (*Tabebuia argentea*). It has large clusters of butter-yellow, trumpet-shaped flowers. The tree itself has corrugated white bark and grayish green foliage that persists throughout the year. It usually blooms in the month of May and is an upright tree and doesn't spread much. The tree

HARDY PALMS FOR TEXAS

Gru gru	*Acrocomia totai*
Queen palm	*Arecastrum plumosa*
Jelly palm	*Butia capitata*
European fan palm	*Chamaerops humilis*
Chinese fan palm	*Livistona chinensis*
Texas sabal palm	*Sabal texana*

FLOWERING TREES

Hong Kong orchid tree	*Bauhinia* sp.
Red bombax tree	*Bombax ceiba*
Golden shower tree	*Cassia fistula*
Floss silk tree	*Chorisia speciosa*
Sunshine tree	*Tabebuia argentea*

my parents planted in 1958 is now about 30 feet tall. Its flowers are mainly at the top, although that might be because it is surrounded by native ebony trees and the top is where the most sunlight hits. Younger trees seem to get blossoms all over.

Another beautiful tree is the floss silk tree (*Chorisia speciosa*), which has clusters of pink flowers. It is a very striking tree with a greenish trunk and spines along the lower trunk. It blooms in fall, usually starting around the first of October. In mild years the foliage will hang on while the tree blooms; in cooler years it begins to fall about the time the blooms appear.

The red bombax tree (*Bombax ceiba*) normally blooms in February. It has big thorns at the base of the tree and large, cup-shaped red flowers that measure 3 to 3 1/2 inches across. The tree has an unusual growth habit. It grows in shelves, but you have to stand away from it for that to be apparent. This is a little more tender to the cold, but it has bloomed well for us for the last four years. It is a striking tree with blooms lasting about a month. In cold winters, the leaves will fall. It just depends on the weather.

Our most prolonged blooming tree is the Hong Kong orchid tree, *Bauhinia*. The flowers are large, deep fuchsia-purple, and highly fragrant. Hummingbirds love them. Here, in Brownsville, it's known as *pata de vaca*, which means "foot of the cow," because the leaves are shaped like the imprint of a cow's foot. This particular variety is a little uncommon. It came to the United States from Hong Kong, where it is now the national emblem.

This is a sterile hybrid and has much bigger leaves and deeper colored flowers than the regular orchid tree, which stops blooming when it sets seeds. Because the Hong Kong variety doesn't set seed, it continues to bloom for a long time. In a good year it begins in mid-October, continues until the end of May, and is literally covered with flowers. It is not a strong, straight tree and rarely has a single trunk. The one in my yard is 35 feet across. It was frozen down in '83 and again in '89 and came back with multiple stems.

The royal poinciana originated in Madagascar. It has scarlet to orange-red flowers that appear in huge clusters. It's somewhat temperamental to the cold, but usually blooms in May and June and sometimes again in late summer if we get good rains. The foliage is similar to that of the mimosa tree. It's more tender than most of the other ornamental flowering trees. Generally, 28° knocks it to the ground.

The jacaranda has blue-purple blooms that are lovely. It's impossible to predict when this tree will bloom. It depends on the individual tree. A tree on one side of town may bloom in spring, while on the other side of town, another may not bloom until fall. I think it's the result of genetic variations within individual trees. Flowering lasts about two months, but varies with the weather.

Wild olive (*Cordia boissieri*) is native to our lower valley. It is cold hardy and drought tolerant, and blooms 9 to 10 months out of the year. It is a small tree, 12 to 15 feet in height and spreads about 12 to 20 feet. The flowers are 1 3/4 inches across.

The bottlebrush has red flow-ers, lightly tipped with gold. The flowers resemble an old fashioned bottlebrush, thus the common name. Golden shower tree (*Cassia fistula*) has beautiful foliage and yellow flowers that hang in long, graceful clusters.

How about the low-growing flowering shrubs?

Bougainvillea and oleander, both of which can get 10 to 12 feet tall, and hibiscus are the old standbys. Also plumbago, trailing lantana, alamanda, red jatropha, and shrimp plant are commonly used.

Plumeria is another large, flowering shrub that is commonly used. It has highly fragrant flowers in white, pink, yellow, and red. Some plants show two or three of these colors combined in one flower. It has large, tropical foliage and succulent stems that may reach 7 to 8 feet in height. This is the flower used to make leis in Hawaii.

Are there new and better cultivars of bougainvilleas now used?

One cultivar of bougainvillea that really stands out is 'Convent'. It is a deep royal purple with large flowers and deep, shiny green leaves. It seems to grow and bloom all the time, regardless of whether or not it gets water. Some bougainvilleas, if they get too much water, will go into a vegetative state and refuse to bloom. 'Convent' does not fall into that category. It is a superior plant. A trio of these that were planted in our yard in 1972 have not been watered in fifteen years. They are always in bloom. Always.

How about hibiscus?

There are many different cultivars on the market. Some are much stronger than others, some are better bloomers, but all do pretty well. Some are susceptible to cotton root rot, since hibiscus and cotton are in the same family. People who have houses on land that was previously farmed with cotton may have real problems.

Some of my favorite varieties include 'von Kleinschmidt', which is a yellow double; 'Crown of Bohemia', which is a quite large double yellow with a red throat; and 'Joan', which is a single gold with a red throat, sometimes tassled in the middle to make it a semi-double. A great pink one used to be called 'Single Pink #10' and is now called 'Seminole'. It blooms constantly and has a beautiful single pink flower.

Are there cultivars or varieties of oleander that you believe are outstanding?

'Shari D' is a beige semi-dwarf, 'Petite Pink' is a pale pink dwarf, and 'Petite Salmon' has soft, coral flowers and is also a dwarf. 'Calypso' is a bright pink tall variety.

Are there shrubs or perennials that you believe are outstanding plants that are underused in the landscape?

I think the native shrub *Xylosma senticosa* falls into this category. I found this a number of years ago about sixteen miles from here. It is robust, has shiny green leaves, is not troubled by insect pests, has no mineral deficiency problems, and resists the coldest weather we have here.

Mountain torch wood (*Amyris madrensis*) is another. It is like a big boxwood with a more open growing habit, but similar small and shiny leaves. It is in the citrus family and has tiny, fragrant flowers. It's so hardy, I think it would survive even a blizzard down here. It gets to be a large shrub or small tree, but you can prune it to keep it as a shrub.

The 'possum persimmon, or Texas persimmon (*Diospyros texana*), is a small tree in the myrtle family. It has exfoliating bark and produces multiple trunks like an old crape myrtle. Its grape-sized black fruit matures in July and August and the birds love it. We counted nine species of birds on it one year, including two species of parrots. It has a beautiful, regal shape. It is the first tree to lose leaves in the fall and first to get them in spring.

What do you use to underplant all these great trees and shrubs?

One of my favorites is the *Dietes*, which is native to South Africa. My parents introduced it to the Brownsville area almost forty years ago. It looks like a small bullrush. It only gets 2 1/2 feet tall and fans out almost like a clump of iris. It is a true iris but not a bulbous or rhizome type. It has flowers larger than a silver dollar, and the flower parts are in threes. The flowers are cream-colored to soft yellow and some have spots of yellow or bright orange with lavender or white centers. It is resistant to wind, heat, and drought and will survive down to 19°. And it's resistant to insects. You get all those qualities thrown in together, and you have one marvelous plant.

Are there common mistakes you see people making over and over?

The most common mistake is putting plants too close together, either because they don't know how big the plants will get or because they just get in a hurry and want to make an immediate effect. Sometimes when I've completely installed a landscape

in which I've left plenty of room for the trees to grow, the home owner will walk up and ask me when I'm going to finish. Usually I can convince them that they will just have to be patient and the plants will grow into the landscape.

A common mistake that people make is putting plants too close together, either because they don't know how big the plants will get or because they just get in a hurry and want to make an immediate effect. You just have to be patient and let the plants grow into the landscape.

Anything else?

I've been interested in plants all my life and I think they are the most wonderful food for the soul. Gardening relaxes you, gives you a diversion, keeps the blood pressure down. Planting a garden is like painting a beautiful picture. Just as an artist picks up a brush and paints with oils or watercolors, you can do the same thing with plants in your yard. A garden is always changing. In forty-four years, I've never not wanted to come to work.

Resources

Display Gardens

Dallas Arboretum and Botanic
  Garden
8617 Garland Road
Dallas, TX 75218
214-327-8263

Houston Arboretum and Nature
  Center
4501 Woodway
Houston, TX 77024

Houston Zoological Gardens
Hermann Park
1513 N. MacGregor
Houston, TX 77023
713-525-3300

Mercer Arboretum and Botanic
  Gardens
22306 Aldine Westfield Road
Humble, TX 77338
281-443-8731

Riverside Nature Center
150 Francisco Lemos Street
P.O. Box 645
Kerrville, TX 78029

Stephen F. Austin Arboretum
P.O. Box 13000
Department of Agriculture and
  Horticulture
Nacogdoches, TX 75962-3000

Organizations

Magnolia Society, Inc.
6616 81st Street
Cabin John, MD 20818

Native Plant Society of Texas
P.O. Box 89
Georgetown, TX 78627

Southern Nurserymen's
  Association
1000 Johnson Ferry Road
Suite E-130
Marietta, GA 30068

Publications

BOOKS

Callaway, Dorothy J. *The World
of Magnolias.* Portland, OR:
Timber Press, 1994.

Dirr, Michael. *Manual of Woody
Landscape Plants: Their
Identification, Ornamental
Characteristics, Culture,
Propagation and Uses.*
Champaign, IL: Stipes
Publishing Co., 1983.

Foote, Leonard and Samuel B.
Jones. *Native Shrubs and
Woody Vines of the Southeast:
Landscaping Uses and
Identification.* Portland, OR:
Timber Press, 1989.

Jacobson, Arthur Lee. *North American Landscape Trees.* Berkeley, CA: Ten Speed Press, 1996.

Jones, David L. *Palms Throughout the World.* Washington, D.C.: Smithsonian Institution Press, 1995.

Native Plant Society of Texas. *Texas Natives: Ornamental Trees.* (*Available for $3.00, P.O. Box 891, Georgetown, TX 78627*)

Phillips, Roger and Martyn Rix. *Shrubs.* New York: Random House, 1989.

Poor, Janet. *Plants That Merit Attention: Volume 1, Trees.* Portland, OR: Timber Press, 1984.

———. *Plants That Merit Attention: Volume 2, Shrubs.* Portland, OR: Timber Press, 1996.

Taylor, Richard B. *A Field Guide to Common South Texas Shrubs.* Austin, TX: University of Texas Press, 1997.

SPECIALTY GARDENING

NATIVE PLANT GARDENING

DENISE DELANEY
Austin: Lady Bird Johnson Wildflower Center

Denise Delaney brings a contagious joy and enthusiasm to her job. As garden manager and senior horticulturist at the Lady Bird Johnson Wildflower Center (formerly the National Wildflower Research Center) in Austin, she is responsible for the Center's extensive native plant collection and nursery operation. She also serves as an environmental educator, giving talks, guiding tours, and writing articles about native plants.

A native of Lincoln, Nebraska, Denise grew up in a gardening family. Her mother and both grandmothers had flower gardens in which Denise began her love affair with flowers and plants. The result of these early influ-

ences was a degree in horticulture from the University of Nebraska and several jobs as horticulturist, including responsibility for the gardens found on the 2 1/2-acre estate of the Chancellor of the University of Texas.

She has been with the Lady Bird Johnson Wildflower Research Center since 1992 and has worked closely with Mrs. Johnson throughout this time.

Indian paintbrush

How do you define the term "wildflower"?

"Wildflower" is really a big umbrella term for all plants native to an area and includes trees, shrubs, grasses, and flowers. The official definition of the Center is that a wildflower is any plant that grew in a particular region of the United States before European settlers arrived. Native plants have evolved and adapted to soil conditions and climatic changes. Our own state flower, the blue-bonnet, thrives only when a specific soil bacteria is present.

Do you find that people are confused by the terms "wild-flower" and "native plants"?

Many people use the word "wildflower" loosely. For example, some people consider "wild-flower" to mean any pretty flower along the roadside, even if it happens to be a plant that must be mechanically reseeded each year. People love the colors of these roadside plantings, but we have to look at the cost.

The high-maintenance approach to roadside plantings and the use of chemicals to accomplish this is expensive both economically and ecologically and defeats the original goal of preserving regional integrity. Educating the departments of transportation across the country remains part of our mission.

Mrs. Johnson, as First Lady, was a strong advocate for the beautification of America. Fifteen years ago, when she and actress Helen Hayes began the National Wildflower Research Center, the goal was to learn how to under-stand, grow, manage, and pre-serve some of the heritage of the land through the use of native plants.

But today, we have evolved into more of an environmental organization. We now study native plant communities in the bigger context of ecosystems. We want to inspire people to become familiar with plants native to their region. Observing plants in nat-ural settings provides clues as to what will work in our own land-scapes.

And finally, we encourage peo-ple to protect the naturally occur-ring ecosystems and natural resources that still exist. We hope that they will work to restore areas when possible, and use native plants in their own gar-dens. We feel that we have grown from encouraging roadside wild-flower plantings to saving the Earth one landscape at a time.

Are all the plants included in the Center's landscape "wildflowers", according to the strictest definition?

About 95 percent of our plants are native to an area within 100 miles of here. In a few locations we have included plants native beyond that range. For example, our wetlands pond showcases some of the moisture-loving species native to East Texas. Another example is a plant such as Texas sage (*Leucophylum frutescens*), which is native to West Texas. It is now prolific in the nursery trade and so useful in the landscape that we use it here in hot, rocky situations, similar to its native habitat.

Our goal here is to continue increasing the diversity of species we use in the landscape and to help create gardens that are interpretations of local native plant communities that can be used as models for our visitors. We would like to be purists, but we have to be realistic as well. We acknowledge that we are not restoring our 4 1/2 acres of gardens; we are landscaping using native plants. Our 40 acres of natural areas are managed as restoration areas, though, including the removal of non-native species and controlled burns in our wildflower meadow.

How do you advise home owners who want to landscape with native plants?

Our first advice is to come here to the Center to see what we have done with our own Central Texas plants. We hope that people will be inspired and will go home to their own regions and discover what their naturally occurring plant communities are. For example, it could be a shady area with a variety of trees, in which case, native wildflowers would be woodland species. Or it could be a prairie area, in which case sun-loving wildflowers would be appropriate. No matter where people live, we send them back to observe their own backyards, for that is the only place to discover what is native to their region.

Observing plants in nature provides clues to what will work in our own landscapes.

We also encourage them to contact our clearinghouse, which serves as an excellent resource center. Information packets are available for seven different regions of Texas and most other states. The packets contain lists of species native to a particular area, and lists of places to buy native plants and seeds. Ideally, you should buy from someone as local as possible. Local native plant societies are also an excellent source of information.

How do you know which plants to put in?

Plants grow in all different kinds of soils, light conditions, and climates. The first thing you need to do is to become familiar with your own property. Look at the soils, the trees, the under-story plants, and light conditions.

Observation will be your greatest educational tool at this point. Notice the mature height of the plants that you want to include, look at wildflowers during the entire growth cycle, and notice which species seem to grow together in nature.

Write down what's there; get help in identifying plants if you do not know what they are. Then preserve what you can, and add to it what you need.

Do you need to amend the soils?

It depends on the site. Here at the Center, we scraped off the topsoil before construction was done. Then we were able to use site-collected topsoil in those sites when we were ready to plant. This worked out really well because we were able to preserve the original seed banks of many species.

We do have areas where we had to bring in topsoil from a different area, and we tried to amend it so that it emulated the original soil as closely as possible. We used various combinations of soil, sand, crushed granite, and cedar flakes.

When you bring in soil from somewhere else, it's difficult to know exactly what will grow well in it. For this reason, I recommend using a mixture of seeds rather than just one species so that the individual species can find their own little niche.

How do you prepare the area for planting seeds?

First, you need to prepare the site properly by getting rid of any unwanted vegetation. Second, you need to choose

STEPS TO NATURAL LANDSCAPING

- Observe what grows in natural regions close to your own yard.
- Identify the plants already growing in your landscape.
- Preserve the plants you can.
- Use native soils where possible.
- Get rid of unwanted vegetation.
- Choose new plants that are native to your region.
- Plant together those groups of species that naturally occur as a plant community in the wild.

seeds appropriate to your area. When you actually sow the seeds, it's important that the seeds come into good contact with the soil.

You can get rid of weeds several different ways. One way is to put black plastic over them to suffocate them out. You have to do this while they are actively growing. You might even want to water them first to stimulate their growth. You can't do this to Bermuda grass, however, because it's too tenacious.

If you are fortunate enough to have a nice stand of native grasses already established in Central Texas, just mow it really short in the fall, rake up the thatch, and plant your seeds. Watering is up to you and Mother Nature.

How do you choose the right species for the area?

Use one of our recommended species lists for your region, then find out what is available commercially. Beginners should choose a mixture that includes species native to their region and ones that will give you color in spring, summer, and fall. Plant height varies, as well as growing cycles, so it's good to choose a mixture of annuals, biennials, and perennials.

It is important to include grasses as well as wildflowers. We suggest that 50 percent to 80 percent of the species be grasses.

This provides support and protection for the taller flowers, prevents soil erosion, and keeps weeds from filling in unoccupied spaces. The grasses are beautiful in fall and winter and provide a good habitat for wildlife.

What are some grasses that you recommend?

Buffalo grass (*Buchloë dactyloides*) is one of the best to use in Texas. Other good species include bunch grasses such as bluestems (*Andropogon* sp.); grama grass (*Bouteloua* spp.); and muhly grass (*Muhlenbergia* spp.).

Can you use European species in the mixture?

We don't recommend it. Many European species will give you flowers the first spring but won't give you repeat bloom because they are not native to the area. European grasses, such as St. Augustine and annual rye, are too aggressive and will outcompete many of the native species.

What is the best time to plant?

This depends on where you live. Fall is often the best time because some seeds need a period of cold before they will germinate. The best time to seed is when the plant would form and drop its seeds in nature. This is difficult when you are planting a wide variety of species, though, so choose a time that seems best for your region, based on the kinds of plants you are using.

How do you plant the seeds?

The most important rule is to have good seed-to-soil contact. The seeds must be touching the soil to get good germination. Mix the seeds with damp sand and broadcast by hand, if possible. Once you have scattered the seeds as evenly as possible, tamp the seeds down into the soil. Be sure to water if rainfall is insufficient. All seedlings need water to grow well.

What if you want to grow a wildflower meadow in your yard but live in a neighborhood with lawn height restrictions?

Look at low-growing species that you can interplant with your turf grass. Our native curly mesquite grass works well because it grows loosely enough for seeds to sprout through it. In one area on our site we have interplanted curly mesquite with horseherb, frog fruit, bitterweed, verbena, and snakeherb, and it is just beautiful. This is a good mixture to use as a lawn alternative.

Are there native grass species that can be used as turf grass?

Buffalo grass is probably the best. It's even available in sod now. You must have full sun to grow this well. It does not need mowing, fertilizing, or supplemental water, once it is established.

Can you include native plants in a formal landscape?

Yes, although how a plant looks often depends on how you maintain it. Plants in a formal garden, whether they are native or exotic, generally need more time and attention to maintain than the same plant would need in a naturalized area. The trick is to find native plants that look formal with little maintenance.

At the Center we have created three demonstration gardens that illustrate a variety of landscape philosophies. Each garden is exactly the same size and is planted according to the same basic design. The first is planted as a traditional landscape using plants commonly found in the nursery trade—shrubs that need pruning, annuals that need replacing each season and so forth. The second garden is planted with native plant counterparts but is still maintained as a formal landscape. And the third is planted with native plants that are allowed to grow naturally with little pruning or maintenance. We will keep

RECOMMENDED WILDFLOWER SPECIES FOR CENTRAL TEXAS

Annuals

Indian paintbrush	*Castilleja indivisa*
Coreopsis	*Coreopsis tinctoria*
Clasping-leaf coneflower	*Dracopis amplexicaulis*
Indian blanket	*Gaillardia pulchella*
Blue flax	*Linum lewisii*
Bluebonnet	*Lupinus texensis*
Tahoka daisy	*Machaeranthera tanacetifolia*
Horsemint	*Monarda citriodora*
Drummond's phlox	*Phlox drummondii*
Black-eyed Susan	*Rudbeckia hirta*

Perennials

Yarrow	*Achillea millefolium*
Columbine	*Aquilegia canadensis*
Butterfly weed	*Asclepias tuberosa*
Lanceleaf coreopsis	*Coreopsis lanceolata*
Prairie larkspur	*Delphinium carolinianum*
Purple coneflower	*Echinacea angustifolia*
Mistflower	*Eupatorium coelestinum*
Maximillian sunflower	*Helianthus maximilliani*
Gayfeather	*Liatris mucronata*
Beebalm	*Monarda fistulosa*
Mealycup sage	*Salvia farinacea*
Ironweed	*Vernonia baldwinii*

track of the resources used in each garden—the time, money and water used—so that we will have concrete evidence of the differences. It should be an interesting project and is one that has already drawn a lot of attention from the public.

We suspect that the butterflies and hummingbirds will go more often to the native plants. The hybridized plants are not bad plants, but they have lost much of their nectar because they have been hybridized so extensively. Something had to be sacrificed for the big or unusual flower forms.

What are some of the benefits of using native plants in the landscape?

Native plants are already suited to the growing conditions of your particular region, and once established, won't need extra watering. Native plants also attract wildlife of all sorts and sizes. For example, using these plants in the landscape will help attract native insects and microorganisms that actually help keep plants healthy and disease free—without the use of chemicals. When using native plants and growing them without chemicals, you are establishing a living plant community, not a garden separate from the surrounding environment.

Perhaps the greatest benefit to gardening with native plants, however, is that in doing so, you are helping to preserve individual plant species as well as helping to reestablish native plant communities, thus contributing to the restoration of regional character.

Resources

Publications

BOOKS

Attracting Wildlife

Burke, K. and J. Wood (eds.). *How to Attract Birds.* San Francisco, CA: Ortho Books, 1983.

Curtis, W. and J. Curtis. *Backyard Bird Habitat.* Woodstock, VT: The Countryman Press, 1988.

Dennis, J.W. *The Wildlife Gardener.* Emmaus, PA: Rodale Press, 1985.

Gellner, S. (ed.). *Attracting Birds to the Garden.* Lane Books, 1974.

Harrison, G.H. *The Backyard Birdwatcher.* New York: Simon and Schuster, 1979.

Henderson, C. L. *Landscaping for Wildlife.* St. Paul., MN: Minnesota Department of Natural Resources, 1986.

Kindilien, C. T. *Natural Birdscaping.* New York: Dell Publishing Company, Inc., 1979.

Kress, S.W. *The Audubon Society Guide To Attracting Birds.* New York: Charles Scribner's Sons, 1985.

Peterson, R.T. et al. *Gardening with Wildlife.* Washington, D.C.: National Wildlife Federation, 1974.

Rothwhild, M. and C. Farrell. *The Butterfly Gardener.* London: Michael Joseph Ltd./Rainbow, 1983.

Schneck, M. *Butterflies: How to Identify and Attract Them to Your Garden.* Emmaus, PA: Rodale Press, 1990.

Landscaping with Native Plants

Art, H.W. *The Wildflower Gardener's Guide, Desert Southwest Edition.* Pownal, VT: Storey Communications, Inc., 1990.

Diekelmann, J. and R. Schuster. *Natural Landscaping, Designing with Native Plant Communities.* New York: McGraw Hill, 1982.

Duffield, M.R. and W. Jones. *Plants for Dry Climates, How to Select, Grow and Enjoy.* Tucson, AZ: H.P. Books, 1981.

Johnson, L. B. and C. B. Lees. *Wildflowers Across America.* New York: Abbeville Press, 1989.

Miller, G.O. and David K. Northington. *Landscaping with Native Plants of Texas and the Southwest.* Stillwater, MN: Voyageur Press, 1991.

Nokes, Jill. *How to Grow Native Plants of Texas and the Southwest.* Austin, TX: Texas Monthly Press, 1986.

Odenwald, N. and J. Turner. *Identification, Selection and Use of Southern Plants for Landscape Design.* Baton Rouge, AL: Claitors Publishing Division, 1987.

Phillips, J. *Southwestern Landscaping with Native Plants.* Santa Fe, NM: Museum of New Mexico Press, 1987.

Smyster, Carol. *Nature's Design.* Emmaus, PA: Rodale Press, 1982.

Taylor, Richard B. *A Field Guide to Common South Texas Shrubs.* Austin, TX: University of Texas Press, 1997.

Wasowski, Andy and Sally Wasowski. *Native Texas Plants: Landscaping Region by Region.* Austin, TX: Texas Monthly Press, 1989.

WATER GARDENING

ROLF AND ANITA NELSON
Katy: Nelson's Water Gardens

As owners of Nelson's Water Gardens, Rolf and Anita Nelson are true believers in the magic of water and the marvelous gardens that can be built around it. Rolf grew up in Brooklyn, New York, and went to the University of Maryland, where he met Anita. Both earned bachelor of science degrees in horticulture there. After graduating, Rolf joined the well-known Lilypons Water Gardens as plant production manager and, when Lilypons decided to open a Texas branch, he and Anita moved to Texas. While Rolf was involved with water gardens, Anita expanded her knowledge and experience by working for a nursery in Houston.

Although twenty years ago water gardening was considered a rather esoteric kind of gardening, today it is one of the hottest areas of gardening in the country. In 1996, Anita and Rolf opened Nelson's Water Gardens, a nursery specializing in water gardens and associated plants and garden art. Although they love working with plants, it is the people that remain their favorite part of the job. "We so enjoy the

people who are our customers. They are so excited about water gardening that they really keep us excited too. The customer's response, the fish, the plants—it all keeps us inspired."

The Nelsons' love of people and gardening, and their skill at bringing the two together, is apparent in their stunning display gardens and the abundance of healthy, happy plants for sale at their store in Katy, Texas.

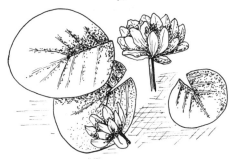

Waterlily

How have the mechanics of water gardening changed: the liners, filters, pumps, and so forth?

When we first began doing this, we only had two options for ponds—fiberglass or concrete. Then manufacturers began making flexible liners out of PVC. These lasted about ten years. Soon they had improved the materials so that the liners lasted about twenty-five years; today liners are made out of rubber and will last up to fifty years.

They are very user-friendly, cost one-third of what fiberglass costs, and are a lot less expensive than concrete. All the liners today are free-form, like a big rubber sheet, and will conform to any shape.

How does a home owner get started?

One of the first things we do with our clients is help them find the best site for their pond and decide what resources they have available for the project. The best site includes as much sun as possible and is as close to the house as possible. You also need to be aware of things such as underground pipes and roof overhangs.

Once the site has been selected, you need to decide what kind of garden you want—Japanese, casual, natural, and so on, and how big you can make it. We always encourage people to make their ponds as big as possible because once the ponds are installed, they always look smaller.

You don't need a professional to put it in for you. As long as it's level and it has a good edging material, such as stone, rock, or slate around it, it will look good.

How deep should the pond be?

All the plants should be put into pots and the pots are then put on the bottom of the ponds, so correct depth is important.

> ## TIPS FOR INSTALLING A WATER GARDEN
>
> - Choose a site with plenty of sunshine.
> - Do not put the pond over underground pipes or under overhanging roofs.
> - Be sure that the pond is level and is approximately 18 inches deep.
> - Make it bigger than you think you want. Once installed in the ground, ponds look smaller.
> - Include plenty of submerged plants.
> - Do not stock too many fish.

Eighteen inches deep is about right. It can be slightly shallower or deeper, but it is more work either way. You need it deep enough to cover the pots, but not so deep that the water lilies and other plants can't grow easily to the top.

What is the smallest pond that you can put in?

We sell a kettle garden, which is a barrel 2 to 3 feet in diameter. It fits well on a deck or patio, is relatively inexpensive, and easy to install and care for. Many people begin with a small garden such as this and move on to something bigger.

For an in-ground pond, probably 12 × 6-foot is the minimum

size you'd want to install, just so you can establish a nicely balanced ecosystem.

Is it necessary to have a pump and filters?

Not really, but many people enjoy the sight and sound of moving water, so they will put in a small pump or bubbler. Filters are not necessary either. All the ponds here at the nursery are set up without filters. We use plants to create a natural balance so that the water stays clear. If it's done correctly, it's really much easier to do it this way, because filters require hands-on maintenance. For larger ponds, we like to build a bog filtration system. This is a natural way of keeping the pond clear.

What kind of plants go into a water garden?

The showiest plants are the tropical water lilies because they bloom so frequently and hold their flowers nicely. Underwater grasses, sometimes called "submerged plants", are essential to help keep the water clean. Hardy water lilies are also nice because they offer a variety of colors not found in the tropical lilies, namely copper, salmon, and some fantastic yellows. Some of the tropical lilies take a long time to emerge in spring and people need to learn to be patient. In April, when everything else looks lush,

these are just beginning to emerge. The water temperature needs to be about 70° before they come alive again.

Other plants might add vertical accent; something such as lotus offers unusual flowers. Lotus are extremely popular, but they are more difficult to grow than water lilies and have a shorter bloom period—only about 6 to 8 weeks—but they are undeniably spectacular.

Some of the tropical water lilies are called "night blooming"; they open at dusk and stay open until mid-morning the next day.

How do you plant a water garden?

Almost all the plants are potted, usually in black plastic pots, which you can't see next to the black liner. Use heavy clay loam in the pot or just regular heavy garden soil. Do not use something that's high in organics (such as composted materials or humus) because you don't want anything that is too light or too rich. Humus will float to the surface of the pond and make a mess. If you have to buy soil, get straight topsoil without any additives.

Underwater grasses should be potted up as well, although there is a native plant, hornwort (*Ceratophyllum demersum*), that is freefloating in the pond.

How do you maintain a pond?

If installed correctly, it takes very little work. During the growing season, go into the pond every two weeks and lift the water lilies, take off the yellowing leaves, and fertilize the plants with 10-14-8 pellets made especially for water lilies. Use one pellet for each 5 quarts of soil that you have in the pot. Water lilies are heavy feeders and if you want the maximum size and greatest number of flowers, you'll want to feed them every couple of weeks throughout the summer.

During the winter, the plants go dormant, so just leave them alone. Repot everything in spring. The root growth is usually so tremendous that you'll probably have to divide the plants when you repot them.

Many of the tropical water lilies will be killed by the cold, so their tubers should be stored indoors through the winter. They can be kept in a jar of water or in damp sand, or if you have a greenhouse, you can overwinter them with the leaves on. In the Gulf Coast region of Texas, virtually all the plants will survive the winters with no problem.

Are mosquitoes a problem?

Not usually. They prefer stagnant water and what you are doing with a water garden is setting up a healthy ecosystem. If you do find that mosquitoes are a problem, one or two fish will readily take care of the situation. If you don't want to have fish, there is a bacteria available that is species-specific for mosquito larvae. This comes in a doughnut-shaped pellet that floats on the water. It is safe and environmentally friendly and will quickly take care of the problem.

In addition, when you install a water garden, you will naturally get predator insects like dragonflies, which are considered the hawks of the insect world; these will help with the mosquito problem.

What do you do if you have an explosion of algae in the pond?

First of all, don't panic. The fish and plants simply don't care. It's an aesthetic issue only. You should begin with an analysis of why you have an excess of algae. It's actually a simple equation. Algae grows because you have free nutrients and sunshine. So if you have excess nutrients, you get an excess of algae. Figure out where the nutrients are coming from. Do you have too many fish? Fish are fertilizer factories. Are you overfeeding the fish? Sometimes if you quit feeding your fish for 4 or 5 days, the algae problem will clear up.

What kind of fish do you recommend for a pond?

One of the basic questions gardeners need to answer before they install a pond is whether they are going to be water gardeners or koi keepers. It's difficult to do both because the koi are large fish and like to dig, which is hard on the plants. For water gardeners, we recommend goldfish only, and a limited number of fish.

Are some tropical water lilies easier to grow than others?

Yes. Viviparous varieties are considered easiest. This just means that they can produce young plants in the centers of their leaves. As a group, they are great for beginners. They will tolerate more shade and cooler water temperatures than others. They're excellent plants and have wonderful colors of blue, purple, pink, lavender, and white.

How do you landscape around the pond?

We like to use "drapey" plants so that the plants around the outside look as if they're jumping into the pond and those in the pond look as if they're climbing out. This bridges the water environment with the land environment.

Many people use rock and stone around the edge of the pond and this actually creates a very dry microclimate. We suggest that people use a selection of xeriscape plants here, such as low-growing succulents around the front of the pond and taller, more shrubby material in the back.

How do you create a natural-looking bog area around a pond?

PLANTS FOR A TEXAS BOG

Dwarf variegated sweet flag	*Acorus gramineus* 'Variegatus'
Cannas	*Canna* sp.
Bog lily	*Crinum americanum*
Dwarf papyrus	*Cyperus isocladus*
Daylily	*Hemerocallis*
Louisiana iris	*Iris* sp.
Blue rush	*Juncus glauca*
Creeping jenny	*Lysimachia nummularia*
Pickerel rush	*Pontederia cordata*
Lizard's tail	*Saururus cernuus*

It's not difficult, and there are several ways to do it. You can create a shelf around the edge of the pond that is much shallower than the remainder of the pond, or put a rock wall across one end of the pond and fill the area behind it with gravel. This not only allows you to plant bog plants but also serves as a filtration system for the pond. Another method is to install a second shallow pond above a deeper pond.

Good plants for a bog area include cannas, which are reliably hardy all the way to Lubbock, classic umbrella palm, lizard's tail, pickerel rush, sweet flag, parrot's feather, Louisiana iris, creeping jenny, and water celery.

DO NOT INCLUDE THESE INVASIVE BOG PLANTS	
Horsetail	*Equisetum* sp.
Aquatic mint	*Mentha aquatica*
Cattail	*Typha* sp.

Any other advice?

A water garden is to be enjoyed. Install it correctly to begin with, don't stock too many fish, and don't overfeed them. Put in as many underwater filtration plants as you can, add a few tropical water lilies, and you'll have a clean, beautiful environment to enjoy for many years.

Resources

Organizations

The International Water Lily
  Society
P.O. Box 2309
Columbia, MD 21045

The National Pond Society
286 Village Parkway
Marietta, GA 30067

North Texas Water Garden
  Society
972-517-3626

Publications

BOOKS

Glattstein, Judy. *Waterscaping—Plants and Ideas for Natural and Created Water Gardens.* Pownal, VT: Garden Way Publishing, 1994.

Heritage, Bill. *Ponds and Water Gardens.* New York: Sterling Press, 1994.

Nash, Helen. *The Pond Doctor: Planning and Maintaining a Healthy Water Garden.* Blacksburg, VA: Tetra Press, 1994.

Robinson, Peter. *The Water Garden, A Practical Guide to Planning and Planting.* New York: Sterling Publishing Company, 1997.

Roth, Susan A. (ed.). *Garden Pools and Fountains.* San Ramon, CA: Ortho Books, 1988.

Slocum, Peter D. and Peter Robinson, with Frances Perry. *Water Gardening: Water Lilies and Lotuses.* Portland, OR: Timber Press, 1996.

MAGAZINES

Water Gardening, The Magazine for Pondkeepers
The Water Gardeners, Inc.
49 Boone Village
Zionsville, IN 46077

Pondkeeper Magazine
c/o Vivicon Productions, Inc.
1000 Whitetail Court
Duncansville, PA 16635
814-695-4325

COMMUNITY GARDENING

BOB RANDALL
Houston: Urban Harvest

Bob Randall has traveled an interesting path to his current position as head of Houston's Urban Harvest. His path took him from undergraduate studies in math and chemistry at Bucknell University to a stint in the Peace Corps in West Africa, then to a master's degree in cultural anthropology at SUNY Binghamton and on to a Ph.D. at the University of California at Berkeley in ecological and cultural anthropology. While at the University of California, he stayed fifteen months on a southern Philippine island studying coconut, tapioca, and fish production.

In both the Philippines and in Africa, Bob became fascinated with how people interacted with their environment to develop a food supply. His conclusion was that a chemical approach to gardening was an old-fashioned, nineteenth-century approach that has been overtaken by the ecological approach of the past few decades.

When he found himself unemployed after the mid-eighties economic collapse in Texas, Bob decided to stay in Houston and use his research knowledge to help people change their lives for the better through gardening and wise land use practices.

He was offered a job with the Interfaith Hunger Coalition, which had begun a small community gardening program to help deal with the million or so people who needed emergency food relief. The big question for Bob became immediately apparent. Why are there a million people in this city looking for food when land is abundant? It was a question that Bob felt was worthy of a lifetime quest—and so began his contribution not only to community gardening within the city of Houston, but to influencing and inspiring other programs in other cities.

Corn

How did the Urban Harvest program begin?

Before Urban Harvest, there was an Urban Gardening program, begun by County Agent Arnold Brown in the seventies. Because of his efforts, the Interfaith Hunger Coalition, a congregation-based anti-hunger organization and part of a broad social service agency, decided to become involved in gardening. The first two gardens were in really low-income neighborhoods and the third was in my own neighborhood in southwest Houston.

At first, in the late eighties, we would grow food and take it to the Food Pantry for distribution. We did not, at first, focus on teaching gardening because most people in need of emergency food supplies do not make good candidates for gardening. For one thing, many of them don't have a stable residence. Quite a few have significant disabilities and 62 percent are children and seniors. This is to say nothing about their not having any gardening skills.

It wasn't just the poor that needed educating, though. Most affluent communities are killing insects and other creatures indiscriminately because they can afford the chemicals to do so. They export a lot of yard waste, destroy the soil, overuse irrigation. There are huge land use problems going on in these neighborhoods, again, because there is no systematic land use education by this society.

I gradually realized that every human being should know what they can do with the land around them—we all have a right to be educated about how to interact with the land.

So we began Urban Harvest, for we believe that a community garden provides an infrastructure for people who want to learn to use the land in a protective, useful way to benefit society. Our aim is to build healthy communities through gardens and orchards. At a very basic level we are an advocacy group that encourages society to take on this task.

What exactly is Urban Harvest?

We are a non-profit association of individuals and small community gardens located within a 25-mile radius of downtown Houston. Our goal is to develop a network of educational gardens and orchards. We also try to support individuals who want to learn how to use land wisely. We have found that people who do well with their own backyards usually want to help the neighborhood school, church, or park have a good community garden.

Our mission statement says that we are building communities from the ground up by promoting sustainable urban land use and horticultural practices to grow food and reduce hunger. We fulfill this mission by working with volunteers from various community groups to plant gardens and orchards.

Urban Harvest has a Board of Directors, over a dozen committees of volunteers, six staff, and a network of eighty-five affiliated community gardens in seven counties of metro Houston.

How is a community garden different from a public garden or a botanical garden?

According to our definition, a community garden is a food garden planted in an area of at least 160 square feet, although most are much larger. It is operated mainly to benefit the community, and this is accomplished in many different ways.

One of the main benefits of a community garden is that it produces food for neighbors in need, or helps improve the diets of people in the neighborhood. These "allotment" or "diet improvement gardens" in a low-income neighborhood can actually improve the quality of life by reducing hunger or improving health by making fruits and vegetables cheaper. Gardening has the added benefit of helping people get exercise as well. In more affluent neighborhoods, a community garden might teach people how to avoid pesticide abuse, lessen pollution, and reduce water waste. Such gardens also provide a place for people to meet and get to know each other and to keep them outside, all of which helps keep crime down in neighborhoods.

Other types of community gardens include donation gardens, where people grow produce primarily to help those in need. Many people down on their luck, including domestic abuse victims, have lives and residences that are too unstable for gardening, even if they knew how. So groups, especially at places of worship, grow and give.

We think having a good community garden within a neighborhood is analogous to having a good library or elementary school. It's hard to see how people are going to develop an interest in the land or in gardening without it.

By growing food and selling it, market gardens (and therefore green markets) can increase income in the inner city, stem the outflow of dollars from a community (by keeping the buying and selling close to home), and improve the quality of produce for everyone. Market gardens provide a steady surplus of food for donation while teaching, by example, how to grow food.

Education gardens are designed to show people what can be done with the land and how it is done. Therapy gardens are designed to help people get physical or mental therapy.

Any of these gardens can be aimed at people of a specific age or with particular needs, such as seniors or those in wheelchairs. Throughout the Sunbelt, schools are realizing that they can use gardens as outdoor classrooms.

Why are community gardens so important?

When I first began working with the issue of hunger in the cities, I blamed several different things—the government, bad food programs, illiteracy. I wasn't sure what was causing it. But there were some factors that just didn't fit. For example, people were putting a lot of labor into mowing lawns everywhere. It seemed that with a very small amount of education, they could plant food instead of lawn grass and with less labor they would have something to show for their efforts. I came to believe that it was more of an issue of education than anything else.

Several generations ago, the people who moved into the city came from farming communities where, if they were not farmers themselves, they at least interacted with farmers and had some information about agriculture. As we have changed from 10 percent urban to 80 percent urban, and are now three or four generations from the farm, we have a situation where no one really knows much about land use anymore. And there is no systematic effort by society to educate them. Just as we teach people to read, we need to teach them about land use as well.

By not using the land for producing food, not only do people not eat well, but they are missing out on a good way to make a living. You can make a decent income from gardening, even if you are illiterate. The twin problems of poverty and hunger in the lowest income sectors is acute, partly because of society's lack of initiative to educate these people about land use.

Hunger is the worst form of low-income food problems. Nearly as bad is the tendency to eat foods flavored with salt, fat, and sugar, all cheap staple flavorings that mask the flavors of bad or highly preserved produce. Cancer, heart disease, and diabetes are all related to the fact that fresh produce is usually expensive due to the high cost of bringing it great distances. At the moment, Houston, which is the fourth largest U.S. city, produces less than 10 percent and perhaps less than 1 percent of its food. At the consumer level, the only plant products grown in the eight-county Metro area are rice, pecans, soybeans, and peanuts.

What are some topics about which you educate people?

We teach them to control pests in a sustainable way, to grow food for their own tables, to compost, to understand and work with the soil. We feel that if learning responsible use of the land is not as important as learning how to read, it's just a notch below.

How many community gardens are you now involved with?

It's hard to tell because they are always changing. But at present, we probably have 80 to 90 gardens that produce food at some level. We are instrumental in helping people set up gardens that they then look after themselves. Our biggest single growth factor is in the schools. A big part of what we are is a free consulting service and many, many schools are now taking advantage of this.

Why do you feel that it is important to have a garden in a neighborhood?

We think that having a good community garden within a neighborhood is analogous to having a good library or elementary school. It's hard to see how people are going to develop an interest in the land or in gardening without it. The difference is that our gardens were not built with school bonds and are not staffed by people who are being paid well to teach. Our schools are more like volunteer schools— or like schools were in the 1820s. We have little funding and only moderately trained volunteers. We hope that in 40 or 50 years things will be different. We feel that it is the contagion approach. We believe that if you put a good garden in a neighborhood, people will want to try it themselves.

Unfortunately, you find that in many cases the gardens fail. There is insufficient support and education for what these people are doing. Because backyard environments vary so much from one to another, it's difficult to give out specific gardening information. But, it is just a matter of getting enough resources and educated volunteers together to make a difference.

How do you go about setting up a community garden?

Good planning is essential. In general, you need adequate funds, a good physical site, knowledge of plants and gardening, and committed people. We teach two-hour classes twice a month on how to begin a community garden, we hand out volumes of printed advice, offer free classes on a wide range of topics,

offer low-cost seeds, maintain a garden book lending library, and offer to come visit sites for free in low-income communities.

STEPS TO ESTABLISHING A COMMUNITY GARDEN
- Good planning
- Adequate funds
- Good physical site
- Knowledge of plants and gardening
- Committed people

How do you choose a site and get started?

There are only a few basic criteria. For our purposes, the site should be at least 50×50 feet and should be sunny for most of the day. You should have a source of water within 200 feet, and it helps if the site is well drained. And be sure that you have free access to this land for at least 3 to 5 years.

Because of our dense gumbo clay, flat poorly-drained terrain, and high rainfall, we believe you will almost certainly have to bring in a good quality topsoil to put on top of the existing soil and will need some sort of framework to keep it from washing away. The frames can vary from four inches to a couple of feet, depending on the amount of soil you put into them. We use solid concrete blocks whenever we can. They are inexpensive and reasonably attractive. We don't use treated wood for these frames because they leach toxic materials and should not be used around food.

In addition, you will need to fence the site and will need tools, cages and trellises, a source of water, and supplies such as fertilizers, mulch, and seeds.

On the average, how many man-hours are needed for maintenance?

It varies according to your site, but a good average is about 90 minutes of maintenance per week per 40 × 5-foot raised bed.

How much food can you actually produce in a community garden?

Again, it varies, but a 40-foot by 5-foot raised bed should produce about 500 servings annually, though we have had community gardeners produce 1,200 servings. Not only is this needed food—it's nutritional food, raised without pesticides. Our goal is not just to help feed people, but to help them learn about nutrition and sustainable land use.

Do you have any suggestions for getting funds to begin a community garden?

Look for a sponsor. Ideally, this would be someone who could provide both funds and volunteers, such as a civic association, local garden club, religious congregation, charitable foundation, or local business. The more people that you can involve in this project, the more impact it will have on the community as a whole.

How much does it cost to get a garden started?

It depends on the size and design of your garden and, of course, on the amount of material that is donated to you. Generally, a garden will cost between $1,000 and $4,000 and will cost a couple of hundred dollars each year to maintain. If you are really on a tight budget you can drastically reduce these costs and can earn funds for maintenance through sale of the produce.

For more information contact:

Urban Harvest
P.O. Box 980460
Houston, TX 77098-0460
713-880-5540
<Urbanharvest@aol.com>

For other community gardening projects in Texas, contact:

Beaumont Community Garden
Roberts Avenue United
    Methodist Church
Beaumont, TX 77701

Galveston/Hitchcock
    Community Gardens
4006-1/2 Highway 6
Hitchcock, TX 77563
409-744-1745 ext. 273

Gardeners in Community
    Development
Dr. Don Lambert
901 Greenbriar Lane
Dallas, TX 75080
214-231-3565

Gardens Minifarms Network
P.O. Box 1901
Lubbock, TX 79408-1901
806-744-8517

APPENDIX

Plant Festivals

Abilene
Iris Trail
April
For dates and information:
Chamber of Commerce
325 Hickory Street
915-677-7241

Amarillo
Mother's Day Iris Show
May
For dates and information:
Amarillo Botanical Gardens

Brenham
Bluebonnet Festival
April
For dates and information:
Washington County Chamber of
    Commerce
314 S. Austin
Brenham, TX 77833

Dallas
Dallas Blooms
March
For dates and information:
Dallas Arboretum and Botanical
    Garden
    Floral display of 200,000 bulbs:
daffodils, tulips, narcissus, azaleas.

Denton
Redbud Days
March

Ft. Worth
Spring Festival in the Japanese
    Garden
For dates and information:
Ft. Worth Botanical Garden
    Traditional Japanese music and
dance, martial arts demonstrations,
etc.

Houston
Amaryllis Society Christmas Bulb Sale
    and Exhibit
For dates and information:
Houston Garden Center

Houston
Environmental Festival
May
For dates and information:
City of Houston Water
    Conservation
713-880-2444

Humble
March Mart Plant Sale
March
For dates and information:
Mercer Arboretum

Nacogdoches
Blueberry Festival
June
For dates and information:
Stephen F. Austin State University
    Arboretum

Tyler
Tyler Rose Festival
October
For dates and information:
Tyler Chamber of Commerce
903-592-1661

Waco
State Garden Show of Texas
For dates and information:
Waco Convention Center
817-772-1270
    *Week-long seminars, classes, exhibits
of plants, seeds, garden merchandise.*

Woodville
Dogwood Festival
April
For dates and information:
Tyler County Chamber of Commerce
201 N. Magnolia
Woodville, TX 75979
409-284-2632

Display Gardens

Alton's
Iris and Daylily Garden
109 County Road 371
Sweetwater, TX
    *Commercial iris and daylily grower.
Gardens open to the public.*

Amarillo Botanical Gardens
Harrington Medical Center Park
1400 Streit Drive
Amarillo, TX 79106
806-352-6513
    *About 3 acres of gardens, including
a good collection of daylily varieties in
the daylily garden and an impressive
perennial collection for West Texas.
Children's theme garden changes every
year—sunflower house in '98.
Expanding to 7 acres by 2002.*

Antique Rose Emporium
9300 Lueckemeyer Road
Brenham, Texas 77833
800-441-0002
Hours: Monday–Saturday 9:00
    AM–6:00 PM, Sunday 11:00
    AM–5:30 PM.
Fees: None.
    *Beautiful display garden showcas-
ing old-fashioned roses as a garden
plant. Includes climbing, miniature,
shrub, and other roses in different
kinds of gardens such as cottage gardens and herb gardens.
    10 miles northeast of Brenham at
10,000 Hwy. 50, 1/4-mile south of FM
390 and Hwy. 50.*

Antique Rose Emporium
7561 E. Evans Road
San Antonio, Texas 78266
210-651-4565
Hours: Monday–Saturday 9:00
    AM–5:30 PM, Sunday 11:00
    AM–5:30 PM.
Fees: None.

Bayou Bend Gardens
1 Westcott Street
Houston, TX 77024
713-639-7750

Hours: Tuesday–Saturday 10:00
   AM–5:00 PM, Sunday 1:00 PM–5:00
   PM.
Fees: Adults $10.00, Students and
   Seniors $8.50, Children (ages
   5-18) $5.00.
   *Formal gardens flanking 1927
   estate. Includes parterre garden,
   English garden, topiary, and butterfly
   garden.*

Chihuahuan Desert Institute
P.O. Box 1334
Alpine, TX 79831

Cockrell Butterfly Center
Houston Museum of Natural Science
713-639-4629
   *Conservatory full of thousands of
   live butterflies, waterfall, tropical
   plants.*

Corpus Christi Botanical Gardens
8510 Saples Street
Corpus Christi, TX 78413
512-852-2100
Hours: Tuesday-Sunday 9:00 AM–5:00
   PM, Monday closed.
Fees: Adults $2.00.
   *Several buildings house collections
   of tender plants such as orchids and
   bromeliads. Bird and butterfly trail,
   includes booklet that helps identify
   plants along the trail. Garden areas
   display traditional bedding plants.*

Dallas Arboretum and Botanic Garden
8617 Garland Road
Dallas, TX 75218
214-327-8263
Hours: 10:00 AM–6:00 PM. Call for
   summer hours.
   *Sixty-six-acre garden on the eastern
   shore of White Rock Lake includes*

*Woman's Garden dedicated in 1997,
4.5-acre formal gardens surrounding
DeGolyer House, large azalea collection, and collection of native Texas
plants.*

Dallas Horticulture Center (formerly
   Dallas Civic Garden Center)
P.O. Box 152537
Dallas, TX 75315
214-428-7476
Hours: Gardens open at all times.
   Conservatory and visitor's center
   open Tuesday–Saturday 10:00
   AM–5:00 PM, Sunday 1:00 PM–5:00
   PM. Closed December 25, 26.
Fees: None.
   *Seven acres of gardens, including
   display areas that emphasize native
   and adapted plants and land and
   resource-efficient landscaping, using
   plants appropriate for both residential
   and urban landscapes. Outstanding
   collection of native Texas plants.
   Library.*

Fort Worth Botanic Garden
3220 Botanic Garden Boulevard
Fort Worth, TX 76107-3496
817-871-7686
Hours: Gardens open 8:00 AM–8:30
   PM. Conservatory open
   Monday–Friday 10:00 AM–8:00
   PM, Saturday 10:00 AM–6:00 PM,
   Sunday 1:00 PM–6:00 PM.
Fees: (Conservatory) Adults $1.00,
   Children 50 cents.
Call for hours and fees for Japanese
   Garden.
   *One hundred fifteen acres includes
   natural areas and formal gardens such
   as a rose garden, outstanding 7-acre
   Japanese garden, conservatory, and
   greenhouse.*

Heard Natural Science Museum and
Wildlife Sanctuary
One Nature Place
McKinney, TX 75069-8840
972-562-5566
Hours: Monday–Saturday 9:00
AM–5:00 PM, Sunday 1:00 PM–5:00
PM. Open year round except major
holidays.
Fees: Adults $3.00, Children $2.00.
*Two-hundred-eighty-seven-acre
wildlife sanctuary, 5 miles of nature
trails. Paved nature trail for wheelchairs. Includes over 240 species of
birds, mammals, reptiles, and amphib-
ians and 150 species of wildflowers and
other plants.*
*Take Highway 75 to exit 38 and fol-
low the brown and white highway signs.
Museum and nature trails are located
1 mile east of Highway 5 on FM 1378,
southeast of McKinney, Texas.*

Houston Arboretum and Nature
Center
4501 Woodway
Houston, TX 77024
713-681-8433
Hours: Trails open 8:30 AM–6:00
PM.
Fees: None.
*One-hundred-fifty-five-acre nature
preserve, 5 miles of trails, changing
interactive educational displays in visi-
tor's center, children's programs.*

Houston Zoological Gardens
Hermann Park
1513 N. MacGregor
Houston, TX 77023
713-284-8300
Hours: 10:00 AM–6:00 PM.
Fees: Adults $2.00, Children (3–12)
50 cents.

*Wonderful display gardens, huge
live oak trees, great use of colorful flowers, bamboos, palms, and tropical plants
to complement animal displays.*

Lady Bird Johnson Wildflower Center
(formerly National Wildflower
Research Center)
4801 La Crosse Avenue
Austin, TX 78739-1702
Hours: Tuesday–Sunday 9:00
AM–5:30 PM.
Fees: Adults $3.50, Students and
Seniors $2.00.
*Beautiful native plant gardens,
interesting architecture and water
catchment system. Gardens include bog
garden, wildflower meadow, courtyard
garden, and both naturalized and
more formal areas. Children's House
is popular with youngsters.*
*From Austin: Take Loop 1 South for
10 miles. Pass Slaughter Lane intersec-
tion. Take the next left on LaCrosse
Avenue.*

Living Desert
Ft. Stockton Desert Gardens
P.O. Box 430
Ft. Stockton, TX 79735
Hours: All.
Fees: None.
*Open to the surrounding area,
located on the south end of old fort
grounds.*
*Garden is under renovation, show-
casing trans-Pecos plants native to the
area; emphasis on small trees and flow-
ering shrubs, cacti, and agave.*

McMurray College Iris Garden
Sayles Boulevard and South 14th
Street
Abilene, TX

For information, contact: Jack Stuard
915-692-2749
Hours: All.
Fees: None.
*Garden supported and planted by
the Big Country Iris and Daylily
So*

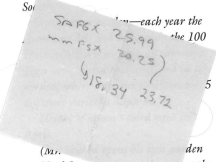

*—each year the
the 100*

*(Mi.   den
on 32nd Street ω .   ng the
month of April and again …   ine
when the daylilies are in peak bloom.)*

Mercer Arboretum and Botanic
   Gardens
22306 Aldine Westfield Road
Humble, TX 77338
281-443-8731
Hours: Gardens and Trails open
   Monday–Saturday 8:00 AM–7:00
   PM, Sunday 10:00 AM–7:00 PM.
   Closed Thanksgiving, Christmas
   Eve, Christmas Day, and New
   Year's Day.
Fees: None.
   *Encompasses 250 acres of East Texas
piney woods along Cypress Creek, about
twenty miles north of downtown
Houston. Within the main garden loop
are collections of gingers, prehistoric
plants, tropical plants, an herb garden,
and a fern garden. Water lilies,
daylilies, and iris make up other inter-
esting collections.*

Moody Gardens
One Hope Boulevard
Galveston, TX
800-582-4673
Hours: 9:00 AM–9:00 PM. daily. Call
   for winter hours.
Fees: Adults $6.00, Children $5.00.
   *Rainforest pyramid (conservatory),
tropical plant displays and gardens,
outstanding facility for horticultural
therapy.*

Riverside Nature Center
150 Francisco Lemos Street
P.O. Box 645
Kerrville, 78029
830-25-RIVER
Jfwest@ktc.com
Hours: Tree trail open dawn to dusk
   daily. Office open Tuesday–Friday
   10:00 AM–2:00 PM.
Fees: None.
   *Includes over 100 native Texas Hill
Country trees, many native wildflowers
and grasses, and a xeriscape garden.*

San Antonio Botanical Garden
555 Funston Place
San Antonio, TX 78209
210-207-3250
Hours: 9:00 AM–6:00 PM every day
   except Christmas and New Year.
Fees: Adults $4.00, Children $1.00.
   *Includes formal gardens, conserva-
tory, children's garden, overlook, and
native areas.*

   *From airport, take 281 South to
Hildebrand exit. Go east on
Hildebrand to N. New Braunfels.
Turn right (south). Continue to
Parland. Turn left (east).*

Stephen F. Austin Arboretum
Stephen F. Austin State University
P.O. Box 13000
Dept. of Agriculture and Horticulture
Nacogdoches, TX 75962-3000
409-468-3705
Hours: Dawn to dusk daily.
Fees: None.
Ten acres alongside La Nana Creek. Many theme gardens, including herb, shrub, and color. Daylily, Texas Heritage, bog, rock, shade, and dry gardens.

TB's Place
1513 Ernie Lane
Grand Prairie, TX 75052
972-602-3975
Hours: Call for hours.
Fees: None.
Commercial iris grower, has garden open to the public.

Tyler Rose Garden
Tyler Parks Department
P.O. Box 7039
420 Rose Park Drive
Tyler, TX 75710
903-531-1213
Hours: Gardens open 6:00 AM–12:00 midnight.
Fee: None.
Over 3,000 shrubs on 24 acres make this one of the largest rose gardens in the United States. Peak bloom in May and October.

Zilker Botanical Gardens
222 Barton Springs Road
Austin, TX 78746
512-477-8672
Hours: 8:00 AM–8:00 PM.
Fees: None.

Opened in 1986, this garden covers 22 acres and is billed as a "feast for the eyes and senses." Includes xeriscape gardens, rose and Oriental garden, butterfly trail.

Organizations

American Begonia Society/Astro
Branch
281-897-0155
(Houston Satellite Branch)
713-946-4237

American Hibiscus Society
P.O. Box 321540
Cocoa Beach, FL 32932-1540

American Horticultural Therapy
Association
Texas Chapter:
Audrey Chadwick
Galveston College
4015 Avenue Q
Galveston, TX 77550
409-763-6551

Austin Community Gardens
4814 Sunshine Drive
Austin, TX 78756
512-458-2009

Austin Pond Society
512-896-6377

Botanical Research Institute of Texas
509 Pecan Street
Fort Worth, TX 76102-4060
817-332-4112 (phone & FAX)

Galveston Garden Club
3427 Avenue O
Galveston, TX 77550

Gardens Minifarms Network
P.O. Box 1901
Lubbock, TX 79408-1901
806-744-8517
Community gardens.

Gardeners in Community
   Development
1018 Gallagher Street
Dallas, TX 75212
972-231-3565
*Community garden and school
garden network.*

Gulf Coast Fruit Study Group
2 Abercrombie Drive
Houston, TX 77084
281-855-5600

Gulf Coast Horticultural Society
4267 S. Judson
Houston, TX 77055

Herb Society of America/South
   Texas Unit
Box 6515
Houston, TX 77265
713-513-7808

Houston Amaryllis Society
713-433-4477

Houston Bonsai Society
Houston Garden Center
713-529-5371

Houston Camellia Society
7815 Burgoyne
Houston, TX 77063
713-781-1996

International Oleander Society
Box 3431
Galveston, TX 77552
409-762-8061

International Palm Society, Texas
   Chapter
13227 Chriswood Drive
Cypress, TX 77429
281-370-7417

Lady Bird Johnson Wildflower Center
(formerly National Wildflower
   Research Center)
2600 FM 973 North
Austin, TX 78725
512-929-3600

Lone Star Daylily Society
281-331-4395

Native Plant Society of Texas
Coastal Region Chapter
P.O. Box 13154
Houston, TX 77219-1254

Native Plant Society of Texas
Mercer Chapter
Mercer Arboretum
281-443-8731

National Gardening Association
180 Flynn Avenue
Burlington, VT 05401

Native Plant Society of Texas
Box 891
Georgetown, TX 78627
512-863-9685

North Texas Garden Railway
   Consortium
<info@ntgrc.org>

North Texas Water Garden Society
972-517-3626
*Meets second Tuesday of the month,
   7:00 PM, at Dallas Water Utilities
   Bldg., 8915 Adlora.*

Southern Garden History Society
Old Salem Inc.
Drawer F, Salem Station
Winston Salem, NC 27108

Texas Association of Nurserymen
7730 South IH-35
Austin, TX 78745-6698
512-280-5182

Texas Botanical Garden Society
P.O. Box 5642
Austin, TX 78763

Texas Dept. of Agriculture
Organic Certification Program
P.O. Box 12847
Austin, TX 78711

Texas Garden Hotline
1-900-990-2900
$1.59 per minute.

Texas Organic Grower's Association
P.O. Box 15211
Austin, TX 78761

Texas Natural Resource Conservation
 Commission
P.O. Box 13087
Austin, TX 78711-3087
512-339-2929

Texas Rose Rustlers
For information, send SASE to:
Margaret Sharpe
9426 Kerrwood
Houston, TX 77080-5428.
<http://www.connecti.com/
 ~cooper/tx-rose/>
 *"An organization dedicated to the
collection and propagation of old
roses."*

Urban Harvest
1900 Kane
P.O. Box 980460
Houston, TX 77098-0460
713-880-5540

Publications

BOOKS

Breneman, Karen Jeppson. *Gardening
 the Upper Texas Gulf Coast.*

Cotner, Sam. *The Vegetable Book: A
 Texan's Guide to Gardening.* Waco,
 TX: Texas Gardener Press, 1986.

Garrett, Howard. *Plants for Texas.*
 Austin, TX: University of Texas
 Press, 1996.

———. *Plants of the Metroplex.*
 Austin, TX: University of Texas
 Press, 1998.

Groom, Dale. *Texas Gardener's
 Guide: The What, Where, When,
 How and Why of Gardening in
 Texas.* Franklin, TN: Cool Springs
 Press, 1997.

Hazeltine, Cheryl. *Central Texas
 Gardener.* College Station, TX:
 Texas A & M University Press,
 1980.

Huber, Kathy and J. Lynn Peterson.
 *The Texas Flowerscaper: A Seasonal
 Guide to Bloom, Height, Color, and
 Texture.* Layton, UT: Gibbs Smith
 Publisher, 1996.

Lane Publishing. *Sunset Western Garden Book*. Menlo Park, CA: Lane, 1988.

Miller, G.O. and David K. Northington. *Landscaping with Native Plants of Texas and the Southwest*. Stillwater, MN: Voyageur Press, 1991.

Nokes, Jill. *How to Grow Native Plants of Texas and the Southwest*. Austin, TX: Texas Monthly Press, 1986.

Peters, Mike (ed.). *The Texas Garden Almanac*. Missouri City, TX: McMillen Publishing, 1996.

River Oaks Garden Club. *A Garden Book for Houston and the Texas Gulf Coast*. 1989.

Smith, Brenda Beust. *The Lazy Gardener's Guide, Upper Gulf Coast*. Houston, TX: River Bend Company, 1997.

Sperry, Neil. *Neil Sperry's Complete Guide to Texas Gardening*. Dallas, TX: Taylor Publishing Company, 1991.

———. *1001 Most Asked Texas Gardening Questions*. Ft. Worth, TX: Summit Publishing, 1997.

Squire, Sally McQueen. *The Complete Guide to Growing Bulbs in Houston*. Houston, TX: River Bend Company.

Taylor, Richard B. *A Field Guide to Common South Texas Shrubs*. Austin, TX: University of Texas Press, 1997.

Urban Harvest Growing Tomatoes in Houston.
713-880-5540

Wasowski, Andy and Sally Wasowski. *Native Texas Gardens*. Houston, TX: Gulf Publishing, 1997.

Wasowski, Sally. *Native Gardens for Dry Climates*. New York: Clarkson Potter, 1995.

Wasowski, Sally and Andy Wasowski. *Gardening with Native Plants of the South*. Dallas, TX: Taylor Publishing Company, 1994.

———. *Native Texas Plants: Landscaping Region by Region*. Houston, TX: Gulf Publishing, 1997.

Water Wise Plants for Houston
P.O. Box 1562
Houston, TX 77251
713-880-2444

MAGAZINES

Gardening the Upper Texas Gulf Coast
Harris County Master Gardeners
Harris Co. Ext. Horticulture
#2 Abercrombie Drive
Houston, TX 77084
Monthly, approximately $12.00.

Neil Sperry's Gardens
P.O. Box 864
McKinney, TX 75070-0864
972-562-5050

Texas Gulf Coast Gardening
P.O. Box 131
Missouri City, TX 77549
713-261-6077

Internet Resources

Howard Garrett
<www.wbap.com>

Extension Service
<aggie-horticulture.tamu.edu/cohort/hansen.html>
<aggie-horticulture.tamu.edu/imagemap/taexmap/smith/smith.html>

INDEX